Gooseberry Patch
From our Kitchen to Yours

ALL-TIME-FAVORITE RECIPES
From

ILLINOIS
COOKS

Dedication

For every cook who wants to create amazing
recipes from the great state of Illinois.

Appreciation

Thanks to all our Illinois cooks who shared their
delightful and delicious recipes with us!

Gooseberry Patch
An imprint of Globe Pequot
246 Goose Lane
Guilford, CT 06437
www.gooseberrypatch.com
1 800 854 6673

Copyright 2019, Gooseberry Patch
978-162093-367-1

Do you have a tried & true recipe... tip, craft or
memory that you'd like to see featured in a
Gooseberry Patch cookbook? Visit our website at
www.gooseberrypatch.com and follow the easy steps
to submit your favorite family recipe.

Or send them to us at:

> Gooseberry Patch
> PO Box 812
> Columbus, OH 43216-0812

Don't forget to include the number of servings your
recipe makes, plus your name, address, phone
number and email address. If we select your recipe,
your name will appear right along with it... and you'll
receive a FREE copy of the book!

ILLINOIS COOKS

ICONIC ILLINOIS

Illinois, the Prairie State, is known for its corn production, its chief crop since pioneer days. Popcorn production also puts the state at the top. Because the state is a big producer, it's not surprising that a favorite snack is popcorn. Chicago-style, though, has its own combination, a mix of cheese and caramel flavors. Illinois is also a top producer of wheat, oats, hay, barley, soybeans, rye and sorghum grain.

Large apple crops come out of Illinois from a number of counties between June and November. In fact, the state is in the top tier of apple-producing states. From some of the same territory, peaches are a hearty crop. Melons grow in the Illinois and Mississippi river valleys.

There's a fishing industry in the state, mostly from inland rivers, such as the Illinois and Mississippi. Many of the foods we identify with Illinois, of course, started in Chicago. It's full of ethnic areas and the foods that came from them. Deep-dish Chicago pizza is a classic that made its debut in 1943, when Ike Sewell introduced it. It's often a must-try for occasional visitors, and Illinoisians have their favorite versions.

In this Gooseberry Patch cookbook, the talented cooks from the Prairie State share their recipes that are dear to their hearts. You'll find everything from Chicago Italian Beef and Old-Fashioned Corn Dogs to Spiced Cranberry-Apple Crisp and Pumpkin Pie Pudding. We know you will love this collection of tried & true recipes from these amazing cooks from the beautiful state of Illinois.

OUR STORY

Back in 1984, our families were neighbors in little Delaware, Ohio. With small children, we wanted to do what we loved and stay home with the kids too. We had always shared a love of home cooking and so, **Gooseberry Patch** was born.

Almost immediately, we found a connection with our customers and it wasn't long before these friends started sharing recipes. Since then we've enjoyed publishing hundreds of cookbooks with your tried & true recipes.

We know we couldn't have done it without our friends all across the country and we look forward to continuing to build a community with you. Welcome to the **Gooseberry Patch** family!

JoAnn & Vickie

TABLE OF CONTENTS

CHAPTER ONE

GOOD MORNING

Breakfast
& Brunch

ENJOY THESE TASTY BREAKFAST
RECIPES THAT WILL BRING YOU
TO THE TABLE WITH A HEARTY
"GOOD MORNING" AND CARRY YOU
THROUGH THE DAY TO TACKLE
WHATEVER COMES YOUR WAY.

BLACK BEAN
BREAKFAST BURRITOS

MEG DICKINSON
CHAMPAIGN, IL

My husband and I love the idea of eating breakfast any time of day.
We love this combination of veggies and cheese!

2 T. olive oil
1/2 c. onion, chopped
1/2 c. green pepper, chopped
3 cloves garlic, minced
16-oz. can black beans, drained and rinsed
10-oz. diced tomatoes with green chiles
1 t. fajita seasoning mix
6 eggs
1/2 c. green onion, chopped
1 T. Fiesta Dip Mix
6 8-inch flour tortillas, warmed
1/2 c. shredded Cheddar cheese

1 Heat oil in a Dutch oven over medium heat. Add onion, green pepper and garlic; sauté until tender.

2 Stir in beans, tomatoes and fajita seasoning. Bring to a simmer and let cook about 10 minutes. Meanwhile, in a bowl, whisk together eggs, green onion and one tablespoon Fiesta Dip Mix.

3 Scramble egg mixture in a lightly greased skillet. To serve, top each tortilla with a spoonful of bean mixture, a spoonful of scrambled eggs and a sprinkle of cheese; roll up tortilla.

Serves 6

FIESTA DIP MIX
2 T. dried parsley
4 t. dried, minced onion
4 t. chili powder
1 T. dried cumin
1 T. dried chives
1 t. salt

1 Mix all ingredients well; store in a small jar. Makes about 1/2 cup.

SUNRISE BISCUIT BUNS

LORI SIMMONS
PRINCEVILLE, IL

Eggs and bacon in a biscuit cup, what fun! I make these for my family and when the kids have sleepovers.

1 In a skillet over medium heat, cook bacon until crisp. Remove bacon to paper towels and crumble, reserving one tablespoon of drippings in skillet. Add onion to skillet; cook and stir until tender, about 2 minutes.

2 In a small bowl, mix bacon and onion; set aside. Spray 8 jumbo muffin cups with non-stick vegetable spray. Place one biscuit in each muffin cup, pressing dough 3/4 of the way up the sides.

3 Divide bacon mixture evenly among biscuit cups. Crack an egg into each cup; top with cheese. Bake at 350 degrees for 30 to 35 minutes, until eggs are set.

Serves 8

1 lb. bacon

1/2 c. onion, chopped

16.3-oz. tube refrigerated jumbo buttermilk biscuits

8 eggs

1/2 c. shredded sharp Cheddar cheese

CRANBERRY-CARROT LOAF

**DIANE WIDMER
BLUE ISLAND, IL**

My grandmother gave me this recipe. I've updated it by reducing the sugar, replacing the oil with applesauce and adding cranberries. I think you'll agree it's still packed with old-fashioned goodness!

2 c. all-purpose flour
3/4 c. sugar
1-1/2 t. baking powder
1-1/2 t. baking soda
1/4 t. salt
1/2 t. cinnamon
1/2 c. carrot, peeled and shredded
1/3 c. low-fat sour cream
1/4 c. unsweetened applesauce
1/4 c. water
2 eggs, lightly beaten
1 c. frozen cranberries

1 Grease the bottom of a 9"x5" loaf pan; set aside. In a large bowl, mix together flour, sugar, baking powder, baking soda, salt and cinnamon. Stir in carrot to coat.

2 Make a well in center of flour mixture; add sour cream, applesauce, water and eggs. Stir until combined. Slowly stir in cranberries. Spoon batter into pan.

3 Bake on center oven rack at 350 degrees for 60 minutes, or until a toothpick inserted in the center comes out clean. Cool loaf in pan for 15 minutes. Remove to a wire rack and cool completely.

Makes one loaf, about 8 servings

GRAMMIE'S COFFEE CAKE

AMY STOLTZ
SAYBROOK, IL

This is a very special recipe to my four sisters and me. Grammie, who was my father's mother, was an exceptional cook and showed her love for us through her cooking.

1 Combine shortening, egg and one cup sugar in a large bowl; beat with an electric mixer on medium speed. Sift together flour, baking powder and baking soda; add to shortening mixture along with buttermilk. Beat until well mixed; pour into a greased 13"x9" baking pan. Top with optional ingredients, as desired.

2 Mix together remaining sugar and cinnamon; sprinkle over batter. Drizzle melted margarine over top. Bake at 350 degrees for 30 to 35 minutes. Serve warm.

Serves 24

1/2 c. shortening
1 egg, beaten
1-3/4 c. sugar, divided
2 c. all-purpose flour
1 t. baking powder
1 t. baking soda
1 c. buttermilk
Optional: raisins, dried fruit, candied cherries, chopped nuts, flaked coconut
2 t. cinnamon
1/2 c. margarine, melted

KITCHEN TIP

An old secret for the flakiest biscuits! Just stir to moisten and gently roll or pat the dough. Don't overmix it.

IVA'S CINNAMON ROLLS

BOBBI JANSSEN
LANARK, IL

When I first met my husband's Grandma Iva, she instantly accepted me as her own granddaughter! She showed me how to make these yummy cinnamon rolls. I have learned that anyone can pass on a recipe, but to watch how a recipe is artfully put together is priceless.

1 t. active dry yeast
3 c. very warm water, divided
1 c. lard or shortening
2 eggs, beaten
1 c. sugar
1 T. salt
8 c. all-purpose flour
1/4 c. butter, softened
1/2 c. brown sugar, packed
1 T. cinnamon

1 Dissolve yeast in a tablespoon of very warm water, 110 to 115 degrees. In a separate bowl, add lard or shortening to remaining water; set aside. Mix together eggs, sugar and salt. In a large bowl, combine yeast mixture, lard mixture and egg mixture; stir in flour.

2 Turn dough into a greased bowl; cover with a tea towel. Let rise for 5 hours; punch down dough every hour. Divide dough into 2 parts. Roll each part into an 18-inch by 13-inch rectangle. Spread butter over surface. Sprinkle with brown sugar and cinnamon, adding more to taste if desired. Roll up, starting on one long side; cut into one-inch thick slices. Place into 2 greased 10" round baking pans. Cover; let rise for several hours to overnight, until double in size. Bake at 350 degrees for about 20 minutes. Cool and spread with Frosting.

Makes 2-1/2 dozen

FROSTING
4 c. powdered sugar
1/4 c. butter, softened
1 T. to 1/4 c. milk

1 Combine powdered sugar and butter; add milk to desired consistency.

PULL-APART MONKEY BREAD

TORI WILLIS
CHAMPAIGN, IL

My kids love this sweet treat! They like to help too. I put the cinnamon-sugar and biscuits in a plastic zipping bag and let 'em shake the bag until the biscuits are all coated.

1 Spray a slow cooker with non-stick vegetable spray. In a bowl, mix together sugars and cinnamon. Sprinkle 2 tablespoons in the bottom of slow cooker. Cut biscuits into quarters; coat biscuit pieces with remaining cinnamon-sugar mixture. Add biscuits to slow cooker; sprinkle any extra cinnamon-sugar on top.

2 In a separate bowl, stir together butter, apple juice and vanilla; drizzle over biscuits. Cover and cook on low setting for 2 to 2-1/2 hours. Uncover and let cool for 15 minutes. Turn biscuits out onto a serving platter; cool for several more minutes before serving.

Serves 15 to 20

3/4 c. sugar
3/4 c. brown sugar, packed
1 T. cinnamon
4 7-1/2 oz. tubes refrigerated biscuits, separated
1/2 c. butter, melted
1/3 c. apple juice
1 t. vanilla extract

PEACHY WAFFLE TOPPING

TORI WILLIS
CHAMPAIGN, IL

*I recently tried this recipe for the first time...after one bite, I thought,
"I've got to share this with all my friends!"*

**16-oz. can sliced peaches
in heavy syrup
1 T. lemon juice
1 T. cornstarch**

1 Strain syrup from peaches into a saucepan. Cut peaches into bite-size pieces and set aside. In a bowl, mix lemon juice with cornstarch. Stir lemon mixture into syrup in saucepan.

2 Cook and stir over medium heat for one minute, or until thickened. Stir in peach slices.

Makes about 2 cups

DUTCH BABIES

JULIE DAWSON
PROSPECT HEIGHTS, IL

*I started making this recipe for oven pancakes for my husband
and myself when we were first married. Now, four kids later, it is a
favorite of all of us. So fast and easy, the kids can help.*

**4 T. butter, divided
4 eggs, beaten
1 c. milk
1 c. all-purpose flour
Garnish: lemon wedges,
powdered sugar**

1 Spray two 8" round cake pans with non-stick vegetable spray. Add 2 tablespoons butter to each pan. Place in oven at 425 degrees to melt; be careful not to scorch. Remove from oven; set aside.

2 Combine eggs, milk and flour; beat until combined. Batter may be slightly lumpy. Divide batter between pans.

3 Bake for 15 to 20 minutes, until sides puff up and begin to brown. Do not open oven while baking. Cut into wedges; serve immediately with lemon wedges and powdered sugar.

Serves 4

JUDY'S FAMOUS BANANA MUFFINS

JUDY MITCHELL
HUNTLEY, IL

Our local newspaper featured me as "Cook of the Week" with this recipe! I found the original recipe many years ago and have revised it over the years. It's a favorite of family & friends.

1 In a large bowl, stir together bananas, eggs, oil and 1/2 cup sugar until combined. Add remaining ingredients except walnuts and remaining sugar; stir just until blended.

2 Spoon batter into 12 paper-lined muffin cups, filling about 2/3 full. Sprinkle tops with walnuts and remaining sugar. Bake at 350 degrees for 20 to 25 minutes, until golden and a toothpick tests clean. Let muffins cool in tin for 5 minutes; remove to a wire rack and cool completely.

Makes one dozen

3 very ripe bananas, mashed
2 eggs, beaten
1/2 c. canola oil
1/2 c. plus 1 T. sugar, divided
1/2 c. quick-cooking oats, uncooked
1/2 c. whole-wheat flour
1/2 c. all-purpose flour
1/2 c. wheat germ
1 t. vanilla extract
1 t. baking powder
1/2 t. baking soda
1/4 t. salt
1/2 c. chopped walnuts

SCRAMBLED EGGS & LOX

JACKIE SMULSKI
LYONS, IL

These eggs are sure to please everyone. We love them with toasted English muffins.

6 eggs, beaten
1 T. fresh dill, minced
1 T. fresh chives, minced
1 T. green onion, minced
pepper to taste
2 T. butter
4-oz. pkg. smoked
  salmon, diced

1 Whisk together eggs, herbs, onion and pepper. Melt butter in a large skillet over medium heat. Add egg mixture and stir gently with a fork or spatula until eggs begin to set. Stir in salmon and continue cooking eggs to desired doneness.

Serves 6

BACON GRIDDLE CAKES

JOSEPH DRUSHAL
CHICAGO, IL

So simple but so delicious! Why didn't I think of this sooner?

12 slices bacon
2 c. pancake mix
Garnish: butter, maple
  syrup

1 On a griddle set to medium heat, cook bacon until crisp. Drain, reserving 2 tablespoons drippings. Meanwhile, prepare pancake mix according to package directions, omitting a little of the water or milk for a thicker batter.

2 Arrange bacon slices 2 inches apart on griddle greased with reserved drippings. Slowly pour pancake batter over each piece of bacon, covering each slice. Cook until golden on both sides; serve with butter and maple syrup.

Serves 4 to 6

COMPANY PECAN FRENCH TOAST

KRISTEN LEWIS
BOURBONNAIS, IL

This recipe makes its own ooey-gooey caramel topping! Since you prepare it the night before, it's a convenient make-ahead when you have guests coming for brunch.

1 In a bowl, combine brown sugar, butter, cinnamon and pecans. Spread in a greased 13"x9" glass baking pan; layer with bread slices.

2 Whisk together eggs, milk and salt; pour over bread. Cover and refrigerate 8 hours to overnight. Uncover; bake at 350 degrees for 45 minutes to one hour. Turn slices over to serve gooey-side up. Serve with syrup, if desired.

Serves 10 to 12

1 c. brown sugar, packed
1/2 c. butter, melted
1 t. cinnamon
1/2 c. chopped pecans
12 slices bread
5 eggs, beaten
1-1/2 c. milk
1 t. salt
Optional: maple syrup

BONUS IDEA

Use a muffin tin in place of individual casserole dishes when making mini pot pies, quiches or savory popovers. So quick & easy!

CHEESY BACON QUICHE

SHERRY GORDON
ARLINGTON HEIGHTS, IL

Quiches are one of my favorite breakfasts, but sometimes I just don't have the time to make one the old-fashioned way. I was so excited when I found this recipe...now I can enjoy a tasty quiche whenever I want!

1 T. butter
10 eggs, beaten
1 c. half-and-half
8-oz. pkg. shredded
  Mexican-blend cheese
1/2 c. spinach, chopped
1/2 t. pepper
10 slices bacon, crisply
  cooked and crumbled

1 Coat a slow cooker with butter; set aside. In a bowl, combine eggs, half-and-half, cheese, spinach and pepper; mix well. Spoon egg mixture into slow cooker; sprinkle with bacon. Do not stir.

2 Cover and cook on low setting for 4 hours, or until a toothpick inserted near the center tests clean.

Serves 8

ILLINOIS FUN FACT

Pepper and egg sandwiches, also called "peppernegg," all one word, started as a Lenten special at a number of Chicago spots. Now it's also a make-at-home sandwich. Between slices of bread, strips of sautéed red and green pepper are served with scrambled eggs and perhaps some cheese. Yum!

SUGARPLUM BACON

BETH BURGMEIER
EAST DUBUQUE, IL

Crunchy, sweet and salty...this bacon is out-of-this-world good! Cook some up for your brunch guests. They're sure to love it.

1 In a bowl, combine brown sugar and cinnamon. Cut each bacon slice in half crosswise; dredge each slice in brown sugar mixture. Twist bacon slices and place in an ungreased 13"x9" baking pan.

1/2 c. brown sugar, packed
1 t. cinnamon
1/2 lb. bacon

2 Bake at 350 degrees for 15 to 20 minutes, until bacon is crisp and sugar is bubbly. Place bacon on aluminum foil to cool. Serve at room temperature.

Makes 8 servings

MOM'S SIMPLE BAKED OATMEAL

JILL DAGHFAL
SUGAR GROVE, IL

Growing up, it was always a treat when Mom made this for breakfast. My dad and all five of us kids loved it. Now I make it for my husband and three children...they love it as well!

1 Combine all ingredients in a bowl; mix well. Spread in a greased 13"x9" baking pan. Bake at 350 degrees for 30 minutes.

Makes 6 to 8 servings

1/3 c. butter, melted
1-1/4 c. brown sugar, packed
3 eggs, beaten
1-1/2 c. milk
3-3/4 c. quick-cooking oats, uncooked
2-1/2 t. baking powder

CHAPTER TWO

LIGHT & LIVELY
Salads & Sides

WITH DELICIOUS FRESH PRODUCE GROWN NEARBY, IT IS A JOY TO MAKE YUMMY SALADS AND SATISFYING SIDES THAT ARE SURE TO PLEASE EVERYONE AT THE TABLE.

CRANBERRY ORCHARD SALAD

CINDY WETZIG
BELLEVILLE, IL

My mother-in-law Jo always made this salad for Thanksgiving and she gave me the recipe. I've been making it for our family for nearly 25 years and it's still a favorite. We enjoy it with our Christmas prime rib dinner too. It's easy to make ahead, the day before...one less thing to do on Thanksgiving or Christmas Day!

1-1/2 c. fresh cranberries
1/2 c. sugar
6-oz. pkg. orange gelatin mix
1/4 t. salt
2 c. boiling water
1-1/2 c. cold water
1 T. lemon juice
1/4 t. cinnamon
1/8 t. ground cloves
1 orange or 2 clementines, peeled, sectioned and diced
1/2 c. chopped walnuts
Garnish: whole cranberries, fresh parsley sprigs or orange segments

1 Process cranberries in a food processor until finely ground. Combine cranberries and sugar in a bowl; set aside. In a separate large bowl, dissolve dry gelatin mix and salt in boiling water. Stir in cold water, lemon juice and spices.

2 Cover and refrigerate until partially thickened, one to 1-1/2 hours. Fold in cranberry mixture, oranges or clementines and nuts; spoon into a 6-cup mold. Cover and chill until firm, about 4 hours. Unmold onto a serving platter; garnish as desired.

Makes 12 servings

ORANGE & HONEY YAMS

VICKIE
GOOSEBERRY PATCH

*You'll love the scrumptious flavor of these sweet potatoes...
and you'll never miss the marshmallows!*

1 Place sweet potatoes in a lightly greased
13"x9" baking pan; set aside. Melt butter in a small
saucepan over low heat. Whisk in honey, orange
juice and cayenne pepper. Drizzle mixture over
sweet potatoes; turn to coat well and season with
salt and pepper.

2 Bake, uncovered, at 400 degrees for 45 to
55 minutes, stirring and basting occasionally with
pan juices.

Serves 4

**4 sweet potatoes, peeled
and quartered
3 T. butter, softened
3 T. honey
1/4 c. orange juice
1/4 t. cayenne pepper
salt and pepper to taste**

KITCHEN TIP

Scoop out oranges or melon halves
and fill with a fresh fruit salad.
They make individual serving
dishes that are very pretty for
a bridal or baby shower.

ARUGULA & NECTARINE SALAD

RITA MILLER
LINCOLNWOOD, IL

You'll love this fruity, nutty salad that's topped with a fresh vinaigrette dressing.

1/4 c. balsamic vinegar

1 T. Dijon mustard

1 T. honey

1/4 t. salt

pepper to taste

2/3 c. extra-virgin olive oil

1/4 lb. fresh arugula, torn

2 ripe nectarines, halved, pitted and sliced

3/4 c. chopped walnuts

1/2 c. crumbled feta cheese

1 Combine vinegar, mustard, honey, salt and pepper in a shaker jar. Add oil; shake until blended.

2 Divide arugula among 4 salad plates; arrange nectarine slices over arugula. Sprinkle with walnuts and cheese; drizzle with salad dressing to taste.

Makes 4 servings

APPLE WHEELS

JACKIE SMULSKI
LYONS, IL

So simple to make and so yummy to eat...the kids will love them! I call this a salad for the kids, but it can be an appetizer too.

1 Combine peanut butter and honey in a bowl; fold in chocolate chips and raisins. Fill centers of apples with mixture; refrigerate for one hour. Slice apples into 1/4-inch rings to serve.

Makes 12 servings

1/4 c. creamy peanut butter
2 t. honey
1/4 c. semi-sweet mini chocolate chips
1 T. raisins
4 red or yellow apples, cored

SUMMER IN A BOWL

ANGIE CORNELIUS
SHERIDAN, IL

We have a large, wonderful vegetable garden every summer. This salad makes excellent use of all those peppers, cucumbers and tomatoes.

1 Combine vegetables, basil, salt and pepper in a bowl. Let stand at room temperature for 30 minutes.

2 At serving time, stir in bread cubes; drizzle with oil. Mix thoroughly; serve at room temperature.

Serves 4

4 roma tomatoes, chopped
1 cubanelle pepper, seeded and chopped
1 cucumber, chopped
1/4 c. red onion, minced
6 fresh basil leaves, shredded
salt and pepper to taste
2 c. Italian bread, sliced, cubed and toasted
3 T. olive oil

CANDIED PECAN CARROTS

NICOLE MANLEY
GREAT LAKES, IL

I created this recipe when I was trying to get my son and my husband to eat their veggies. They aren't too fond of carrots, but this is one dish they don't pass up!

1/4 c. butter
5 T. brown sugar, packed
1 t. nutmeg
2 t. cinnamon
1/4 c. chopped pecans
16-oz. pkg. frozen carrots, cooked

1 Melt butter in a saucepan over medium heat; stir in brown sugar. Stir until dissolved. Add remaining ingredients except carrots; stir well.

2 Combine brown sugar mixture and cooked carrots in an ungreased 2-1/2 quart casserole dish. Bake, uncovered, at 350 degrees for 15 to 20 minutes.

Makes 4 to 6 servings

KITCHEN TIP

Make extra salad dressing and keep in the refrigerator for a last-minute salad topper.

CREAMY MASHED POTATOES

LORI SIMMONS
PRINCEVILLE, IL

I was raised on homemade mashed potatoes and still make them for my family. They're so much more flavorful than instant!

1 Cover potatoes with water in a saucepan over medium-high heat. Boil until tender; drain.

2 Mash potatoes until creamy. Stir in remaining ingredients until well blended.

Serves 4

3 to 4 potatoes, peeled and cubed
1/4 c. butter, softened
1/4 c. milk
1/4 t. salt
1/8 t. pepper

TOMATO-BASIL PASTA BAKE

JENNIE GIST
GOOSEBERRY PATCH

Your family will love the fresh taste of the homemade pasta sauce... it's simple to make using canned tomatoes.

1 In a large skillet, sauté onion and garlic in butter until onion is tender. Stir in tomatoes with juice and seasonings. Bring to a boil; reduce heat. Simmer, uncovered, for about 20 minutes. Stir in capers, if using; remove from heat.

2 Meanwhile, measure out half the spaghetti, reserving the rest for another recipe. Cook according to package directions. Drain spaghetti and add to skillet; toss to coat with sauce. Spoon into a lightly greased 9"x9" baking pan. Sprinkle with cheese. Bake at 400 degrees for 5 to 8 minutes, or until bubbly and cheese is melted.

Serves 4

2/3 c. onion, chopped
2 cloves garlic, minced
2 T. butter
28-oz. can diced tomatoes with Italian herbs
2 T. fresh basil, snipped
1/2 t. sugar
1/4 t. pepper
Optional: 1 T. capers, drained
8-oz. pkg. thin spaghetti, uncooked and divided
1/2 c. shredded mozzarella cheese

FRIED APPLES & ONIONS

DAWN HOBBS
DEKALB, IL

My grandmother used to eat onions like apples...this dish combines the two favorites together! It goes well with fried pork chops.

2 c. onion, sliced
2 T. butter
2 c. Granny Smith apples, peeled, cored and sliced
1/2 c. water
1 t. salt
1/2 t. dried thyme

1 In a skillet over medium-low heat, cook onions slowly in butter until tender. Add apples, water, salt and thyme.

2 Cover and cook until apples are soft, about 5 to 10 minutes. Uncover; continue cooking until all water is absorbed and apples and onions are lightly golden.

Serves 4 to 6

SPOON BREAD FLORENTINE

JO ANN
GOOSEBERRY PATCH

Deliciously different and so simple to make.

10-oz. pkg. frozen chopped spinach, thawed and drained
6 green onions, sliced
1 red pepper, chopped
5-1/2 oz. pkg. cornbread mix
4 eggs, beaten
1/2 c. butter, melted
1 c. cottage cheese
1-1/4 t. seasoned salt

1 Combine all ingredients in a large bowl; mix well. Spoon into a lightly greased slow cooker. Cover, with lid slightly ajar to allow moisture to escape.

2 Cook on low setting for 3 to 4 hours, or on high setting for 1-3/4 to 2 hours, until edges are golden and a knife tip inserted in center tests clean.

Makes 8 servings

GREEN BEANS ALMONDINE

MICHELLE CAMPEN
PEORIA, IL

I just love green beans and I'm always looking for new ways to prepare them. This recipe is a new favorite.

1 Place beans in a stockpot of salted boiling water and cook for 2 minutes. Drain and run under cold water. Drain again. Set aside to dry on paper towels.

2 Cook bacon in a large, heavy skillet over medium-high heat until crisp. Drain all but 2 tablespoons of drippings from skillet. Add garlic, seasoning and almonds to skillet; sauté one minute. Stir in beans and sauté until beans are crisp-tender. Drizzle soy sauce over beans; stir and serve immediately.

Serves 8

2 lbs. green beans, trimmed and halved

8 slices bacon, chopped

2 cloves garlic, thinly sliced

1 t. Italian seasoning

1 c. sliced almonds

1 t. soy sauce

KITCHEN TIP

Keep slow-cooked food hot for carry-ins...wrap the crock in several layers of newspaper, then set in an insulated cooler. Food will stay warm for up to 2 hours.

GRILLED VEGETABLE SALAD

JO ANN
GOOSEBERRY PATCH

I received this terrific recipe from a cooking class.

1 ear corn, husked
16 spears asparagus, trimmed
16 green onions, trimmed
8 roma tomatoes, halved
1 bulb fennel, thinly sliced
2 to 3 T. olive oil
salt and pepper to taste
1 c. couscous, cooked
6-oz. pkg. spring greens
Garnish: chopped fresh basil, parsley and/or mint

1 Place all vegetables in a grill basket. Drizzle with oil; season with salt and pepper. Place basket on a grate over high heat. Cook until tender, about 5 to 10 minutes, turning occasionally. Remove grill basket from grill; cool.

2 Slice corn kernels off cob; cut other vegetables into bite-size pieces. Combine all vegetables in a large salad bowl. Add couscous and greens. Add Vinaigrette to taste; toss to mix. Garnish with herbs.

Serves 4 to 6

VINAIGRETTE

1/2 c. olive oil
1/4 c. lemon juice
1 T. Dijon mustard
salt and pepper to taste

1 Whisk together all ingredients in a bowl, blending well.

HEAVENLY RICE

LINDA ROBINSON
DIAMOND, IL

My family enjoyed this yummy dish at every holiday for many years. Recently we were invited to my cousin's house for dinner, so I made Heavenly Rice and took it in the same bowl that my grandmother and mom had served it in. It brought back so many memories of family and togetherness!

1 Place dry gelatin mix, powdered sugar and vanilla in a large bowl; add boiling water and stir well. Add pineapple and rice; mix well.

2 With an electric mixer on high setting, whip cream until stiff peaks form. Fold whipped cream into gelatin mixture. Spoon into a serving bowl; cover and refrigerate for 2 hours to overnight.

Makes 10 servings

3-oz. pkg. strawberry gelatin mix

1/2 c. powdered sugar

1 t. vanilla extract

1/2 c. boiling water

2 c. crushed pineapple, drained

1 c. cooked long-cooking rice, cooled

1 pt. whipping cream

ITALIAN-STYLE VEGETABLES

**TORI WILLIS
CHAMPAIGN, IL**

*A scrumptious side dish, or for a meatless main, ladle the
vegetable mixture over cooked pasta or squares of polenta.*

**1 eggplant, peeled and
cut in 1-inch cubes**

**2 to 3 zucchini, halved
lengthwise and sliced
1/2-inch thick**

1 t. salt

1 T. olive oil

3/4 lb. sliced mushrooms

1 onion, sliced thinly

4 roma tomatoes, sliced

2 c. tomato sauce

1 t. dried oregano

salt and pepper to taste

**1-1/2 c. shredded Italian-
blend cheese**

1 In a bowl, toss eggplant and zucchini with salt.
Place in a large colander; set over bowl to drain for
one hour. Squeeze out excess moisture. Heat oil
in a large skillet over medium heat. Add eggplant,
zucchini, mushrooms and onion; sauté just until
tender.

2 In a slow cooker, layer 1/3 each of vegetable
mixture, tomatoes, tomato sauce, seasonings and
cheese. Repeat layers 2 more times, ending with
cheese on top. Cover and cook on low setting for
6 to 8 hours, until vegetables are tender.

Serves 6 to 8

MINNIE'S CORN SALAD

BARBARA COOPER
ORION, IL

A friend at church shared this salad recipe with me. It's so easy, colorful and delicious!

1 Combine corn, peppers, onion, cheese and mayonnaise in a serving bowl. Stir well; cover and refrigerate until serving time. Add crushed chips to taste just before serving.

Makes 6 to 8 servings

2 15-oz. cans corn, drained

15-oz. can sweet corn & diced peppers, drained

1/2 red pepper, diced

1/2 green pepper, diced

1 red onion, diced

1-1/2 to 2 c. shredded Cheddar cheese

1 c. mayonnaise

5-oz. pkg. chili cheese corn chips, crushed

MINTY MELON SALAD

VICKIE
GOOSEBERRY PATCH

The spicy, fresh mint really brings out the sweetness of the juicy melon in this bright & cheery salad.

1 Combine water, sugar, juice and mint in a saucepan; bring to a boil. Boil for 2 minutes, stirring constantly. Remove from heat; cover and cool completely. Combine fruit in a large bowl.

2 Pour cooled dressing over fruit; stir until well coated. Cover and chill for at least 2 hours, stirring occasionally. Drain liquid before serving. Garnish with fresh mint sprigs.

Serves 10

1 c. water

3/4 c. sugar

3 T. lime juice

1-1/2 t. fresh mint, chopped

5 c. watermelon, cubed

3 c. cantaloupe, cubed

3 c. honeydew, cubed

2 c. nectarines, pitted and sliced

1 c. blueberries

Garnish: fresh mint sprigs

MINTED BABY CARROTS

TORI WILLIS
CHAMPAIGN, IL

Mint is so easy to grow...keep some growing in a sunny spot by the kitchen door, and you can whip up these yummy carrots anytime.

1/2 lb. baby carrots
2 T. butter
salt and pepper to taste
1 T. lemon zest, minced
1 T. brown sugar, packed
2 t. fresh mint, minced

1 In a stockpot of boiling water, cook the carrots 5 minutes. Remove from heat and drain. Melt butter in a skillet over medium-high heat. Stir in carrots; cook until crisp-tender. Season with salt and pepper as desired. Combine remaining ingredients and sprinkle over individual servings.

Makes 4 servings

PARMESAN BAKED TOMATOES

JILL BURTON
GOOSEBERRY PATCH

This is super in the summer when you have fresh-from-the-garden tomatoes!

1/4 c. bread crumbs
3 T. grated Parmesan cheese
2 T. olive oil, divided
1 t. garlic, minced
5 tomatoes

1 Stir together bread crumbs, Parmesan cheese, one tablespoon olive oil and garlic. Using a sharp knife, slice the top 1/3 from each tomato and place cut-side up in an 11"x7" baking dish. Divide bread crumb mixture equally among each tomato and sprinkle over tomato tops.

2 Drizzle tops with remaining olive oil, then bake at 450 degrees for 8 to 10 minutes or until bread crumbs are toasted.

Makes 5 servings

SAUTÉED ZUCCHINI & YELLOW SQUASH

ANDREA SNYDER
CARTERVILLE, IL

When I was growing up, my mother always used to make this dish for us. I have continued to make it for my children, who often have a second helping or three! It is so good and quick.

1 Melt butter in a skillet over medium heat. Add squash; sprinkle with garlic. Stir; sauté until crisp-tender. If desired, cover to speed up cooking a little. Just before serving, sprinkle with cheese. Let stand until melted.

Makes 4 servings

3 T. butter
2 to 3 zucchini and/or yellow squash, thinly sliced
2 cloves garlic, minced
1/2 c. grated Parmesan cheese

SCALLOPED PINEAPPLE

DOLLIE ISAACSON
DANVILLE, IL

A friend shared this recipe when we were invited to her house for a hot dog roast. Now it's a favorite for family gatherings.

1 Beat together eggs and sugar in a large bowl; stir in remaining ingredients in order given.

2 Pour into a greased 11"x7" baking pan. Bake, uncovered, at 350 degrees for 40 minutes.

Serves 6 to 8

3 eggs
2 c. sugar
1 c. butter, melted
3/4 c. milk
20-oz. can pineapple chunks, drained
8 slices white bread, torn

PARTY-TIME BEANS

KAREN MCCARTY
CHAMPAIGN, IL

I make these beans often, and they're always a hit...perfect for potlucks, parties, celebrations and get-togethers. All the different types of beans make them a welcome alternative to the same old baked beans.

1-1/2 c. catsup
1 onion, chopped
1 green pepper, chopped
1 red pepper, chopped
1/2 c. water
1/2 c. brown sugar, packed
2 bay leaves
2 to 3 t. cider vinegar
1 t. dry mustard
1/8 t. pepper
16-oz. can kidney beans, drained and rinsed
15.8-oz. can Great Northern beans, drained and rinsed
14-1/2 oz. can lima beans, drained and rinsed
15-1/2 oz. can black beans, drained and rinsed
16-oz. can black-eyed peas, drained and rinsed

1 In a slow cooker, combine catsup, onion, green and red peppers, water, brown sugar, bay leaves, vinegar, mustard and pepper; mix well. Add beans and peas to slow cooker; mix well.

2 Cover and cook on low setting for 5 to 7 hours, until onion and peppers are tender and beans are heated through. Remove bay leaves before serving.

Serves 12 to 14

QUICK & EASY PARMESAN ASPARAGUS

PAULA SMITH
OTTAWA, IL

From oven to table in only 15 minutes!

1 Add asparagus and one inch of water in a large skillet. Bring to a boil. Reduce heat; cover and simmer for 5 to 7 minutes, until crisp-tender.

2 Drain and arrange asparagus in a greased 13"x9" baking pan. Drizzle with butter; sprinkle with Parmesan cheese, salt and pepper. Bake, uncovered, at 350 degrees for 10 to 15 minutes, until cheese melts.

Serves 8 to 10

4 lbs. asparagus, trimmed
1/4 c. butter, melted
2 c. shredded Parmesan cheese
1 t. salt
1/2 t. pepper

ILLINOIS FUN FACT

You don't have to be Canadian to like poutine, which is popular in Illinois. It consists of a mixture of French fries and cheese curds topped with brown gravy. It's an import from Quebec.

RIPE TOMATO TART

DARLENE LOHRMAN
CHICAGO, IL

Fresh roma tomatoes are available year 'round so you can enjoy this summery-tasting pie anytime.

9-inch pie crust
1-1/2 c. shredded mozzarella cheese, divided
4 roma tomatoes, cut into wedges
3/4 c. fresh basil, chopped
4 cloves garlic, minced
1/2 c. mayonnaise
1/2 c. grated Parmesan cheese
1/8 t. white pepper

1 Line an ungreased 9" tart pan with pie crust; press crust into fluted sides of pan and trim edges.

2 Bake at 450 degrees for 5 to 7 minutes; remove from oven. Sprinkle with 1/2 cup mozzarella cheese; let cool on a wire rack. Combine remaining ingredients; mix well and fill crust. Reduce heat to 375 degrees; bake for about 20 minutes, or until bubbly on top.

Makes 6 servings

ROTINI SALAD WITH CRABMEAT

TONI GROVES
BENLD, IL

A special friend gave me this delicious recipe years ago. Whenever I make it for a get-together, someone is sure to ask for the recipe.

1 Cook pasta according to package directions. Drain; rinse with cold water and transfer to a serving bowl. Add remaining ingredients except salad dressing; mix gently.

2 Add desired amount of salad dressing; toss to coat well. Cover and refrigerate until chilled.

Serves 10 to 12

12-oz. pkg. rainbow rotini pasta, uncooked

9-oz. pkg. frozen peas, thawed

6-oz. jar marinated artichokes, drained and chopped

4-oz. can sliced black olives, drained

1 red onion, sliced

2 ripe tomatoes, chopped

1 green onion, sliced

16-oz. pkg. crabmeat, chopped

24-oz. bottle zesty Italian salad dressing

BONUS IDEA

Set a regular dinner theme for each night of the week. Choose Italian Night, Soup & Salad Night or Mexican Night, based on your family's favorites. You'll be creating memories together and meal planning is a snap!

CHAPTER THREE

GOOD & TASTY

Soups & Sandwiches

NO MATTER WHAT THE WEATHER,

YOU CAN ALWAYS COZY UP

WITH A BOWL OF SOUL-SOOTHING

SOUP AND A HEARTY SANDWICH

FOR A SATISFYING LUNCH OR

QUICK-TO-MAKE DINNER.

CHICAGO ITALIAN BEEF

HEATHER PORTER
VILLA PARK, IL

If you come from Chicago you know Italian beef. Serve with chewy, delicious Italian rolls and top with some of the gravy from the slow cooker...the taste is out of this world!

4 to 5-lb. beef rump roast or bottom round roast

16-oz. jar pepperoncini

16-oz. jar mild giardiniera mix in oil

14-oz. can beef broth

1.05-oz. pkg. Italian salad dressing mix

10 to 14 Italian rolls, split

1 Place roast in a large slow cooker. Top with undrained pepperoncini and giardeniera; pour in broth and sprinkle with dressing mix.

2 Cover and cook on low setting for 6 to 8 hours. Reserving liquid in slow cooker, shred beef with 2 forks. To serve, top rolls with beef and some of the liquid and vegetables from slow cooker.

Serves 10 to 14

SHRIMPLY WONDERFUL BAGEL SANDWICHES

JENNIFER GUBBINS
HOMEWOOD, IL

Serve on mini bagels for perfect bite-size sandwiches.

3-oz. pkg. cream cheese, softened

4-1/4 oz. can tiny shrimp, drained and rinsed

2 T. mayonnaise

1 T. lemon juice

1/2 t. dill weed

4 bagels, split and toasted

1 avocado, peeled, pitted and sliced

1 Mix cream cheese, shrimp, mayonnaise, lemon juice and dill weed. Spread mixture onto 4 bagel halves. Top with avocado slices and remaining bagel halves.

Makes 4

OLD-FASHIONED CORN DOGS

SHARRY MURAWSKI
OAK FOREST, IL

You just can't beat a homemade corn dog! My mom used to make us these corn dogs when I was young. Now, I don't make them too often, but when the mood strikes...these really hit the spot.

1 In a large bowl, mix together cornmeal, flour, baking powder, milk, salt, sugar and egg until smooth; set aside.

2 Pat hot dogs dry. Insert a stick into each hot dog, leaving some exposed for a handle. Heat about 2 inches of oil to 365 degrees in a deep saucepan over medium-high heat. Roll hot dogs in batter until evenly coated. Fry hot dogs in oil, a few at a time, until golden on all sides. Drain on paper towels before serving.

Makes 8

1/2 c. cornmeal
1-1/2 c. all-purpose flour
4 t. baking powder
1 c. milk
2 t. salt
1/4 c. sugar
1 egg, beaten
8 hot dogs
8 wooden craft sticks
oil for deep frying

CHICKEN SALAD CROISSANTS

ARLENE SMULSKI
LYONS, IL

This isn't your ordinary chicken salad. This version stirs in raisins, almonds and dried cranberries. These sandwiches are a treat for a quick supper or a casual weekend lunch.

2 c. cooked chicken, cubed

1/3 c. celery, diced

1/4 c. raisins

1/4 c. dried cranberries

1/4 c. sliced almonds

2/3 c. mayonnaise

1/8 t. pepper

1 T. fresh parsley, minced

1 t. mustard

1 T. lemon juice

4 croissants, split in half horizontally

4 lettuce leaves

1 Combine all ingredients except croissants and lettuce leaves in a large mixing bowl; mix well. Cover and chill 2 to 3 hours.

2 Place one lettuce leaf and about 3/4 cup mixture on the bottom half of each croissant; top with remaining croissant halves.

Serves 4

SANDY'S BBQ PULLED PORK WITH ROOT BEER

DIANE HOLLAND
GALENA, IL

A favorite easy recipe given to me by my sister-in-law Sandy. It's terrific when you're having company and don't want to stay in the kitchen all day.

1 Place pork roast in a slow cooker; add enough root beer to cover roast. Cover and cook on low setting for 8 to 9 hours, until pork is very tender. Remove pork from slow cooker to a large bowl; drain and discard root beer and drippings.

2 Shred pork with 2 forks; return to slow cooker. Add barbecue sauce to desired consistency; cover and warm through. To serve, spoon pork and sauce onto hoagie buns.

Serves 8 to 12

3 to 4-lb. pork shoulder roast

2-ltr. bottle favorite root beer

18-oz. jar favorite barbecue sauce

8 to 12 hoagie buns, split

ROSEMARY-DIJON CHICKEN CROISSANTS

JO ANN
GOOSEBERRY PATCH

Pair with fruit salad cups and sweet tea for a delightful brunch.

1 Combine all ingredients except lettuce and croissants in a large bowl; mix well.

2 Arrange lettuce leaves inside croissants, if desired; spread with chicken mixture.

Makes 10 mini sandwiches

3 c. cooked chicken breast, chopped

1/3 c. green onions, chopped

1/4 c. toasted almonds, coarsely chopped

1/4 c. plain yogurt

1/4 c. mayonnaise

1 t. fresh rosemary, chopped

1 t. Dijon mustard

1/8 t. salt

1/8 t. pepper

Optional: leaf lettuce

10 mini croissants, split

WANDA'S WIMPIES

WANDA LEUTY
SWANSEN, IL

An easy Sloppy Joe recipe for busy parents and grandparents.

1-1/2 lbs. lean ground beef
salt and pepper to taste
10-3/4 oz. can tomato soup
1/2 c. tangy-flavored catsup
6 to 8 sandwich buns

1 Brown beef in a heavy saucepan; salt and pepper to taste. Add soup and catsup; reduce heat and simmer until thick. Spoon onto buns to serve.

Makes 6 to 8 servings.

BEEFY TACO POCKETS

SHERRY GORDON
ARLINGTON HEIGHTS, IL

My kids love homemade tacos! They ask for tacos so often that I thought I would give this recipe a try, just for a change. Now these neat-to-eat pockets are a family favorite too.

1 lb. ground beef
1-1/4 oz. pkg. taco seasoning mix
2/3 c. water
1-1/2 c. chunky salsa, divided
16.3-oz. can refrigerated jumbo biscuits
1 c. shredded Mexican-blend cheese blend, divided
Garnish: sour cream

1 Brown beef in a skillet over medium heat; drain. Stir in seasoning mix, water and 1/2 cup salsa. Simmer for 2 to 3 minutes, until thickened. Separate biscuits; flatten into 6-inch circles.

2 Spoon beef mixture and one tablespoon cheese onto each biscuit. Fold biscuits in half over filling; press to seal well. Arrange on a lightly greased baking sheet. Bake at 375 degrees for 9 to 14 minutes, until golden. Garnish with remaining cheese, salsa and sour cream.

Makes 8

BARBECUE BEEF CHILI

SHERRY GORDON
ARLINGTON HEIGHTS, IL

This is a different kind of chili that my husband loves. He works outdoors most of the day, so his face lights up when he comes in from the cool fall air after work and smells this chili simmering away in the slow cooker.

1 In a bowl, combine seasonings. Rub seasoning mixture on all sides of brisket; place in a slow cooker. In a separate bowl, combine remaining ingredients except beans; mix well and spoon over brisket.

2 Cover and cook on high setting for 5 to 6 hours, until brisket is very tender. Remove brisket from slow cooker; shred with 2 forks. Return shredded brisket to slow cooker; reduce to low setting. Stir in beans; cover and cook for one hour, or until heated through.

Serves 10 to 12

7 t. chili powder
1 T. garlic powder
2 t. celery seed
1 t. pepper
1/2 t. cayenne pepper
4-lb. beef brisket
1 green pepper, chopped
1 onion, chopped
12-oz. bottle chili sauce
1/2 c. barbecue sauce
1/4 c. Worcestershire sauce
1 c. catsup
1/3 c. brown sugar, packed
1/4 c. cider vinegar
1 t. dry mustard
15-1/2 oz. can hot chili beans
15-1/2 oz. can Great Northern beans, drained and rinsed

GRANDMA HALLIE'S SPICY CHILI

ASHLEY HULL
VIRDEN, IL

This recipe is from my Great-Grandma Hallie. I am so glad I actually have one of her recipes written down! She would make the best food and say, "Honey, it's all up here," meaning she memorized all her recipes. This recipe shows what a wonderful cook she was!

2 lbs. ground beef
1/4 c. dried, minced onion
2 t. salt
2 10-3/4 oz. cans tomato soup
2 16-oz. cans kidney beans
2-1/2 c. water
1 t. Worcestershire sauce
2 T. butter, sliced
3 T. chili powder

1 In a large soup pot, brown beef over medium heat; drain. Add remaining ingredients; reduce heat to medium-low. Simmer for 45 minutes, stirring occasionally.

Makes 8 to 10 servings

CHILI-WEATHER CHILI

MARY JO BABIARZ
SPRING GROVE, IL

Serve with ciabatta bread and cheese for a complete meal.

1 lb. ground beef
2 T. onion, diced
15-3/4 oz. can chili beans with chili sauce
8-1/4 oz. can refried beans
8-oz. can tomato sauce
8-oz. jar salsa
Garnish: shredded cheese

1 Brown beef and onion together in a large stockpot; drain. Add remaining ingredients. Bring to a boil and reduce heat to medium; add 1/2 cup water if mixture is too thick.

2 Cover and simmer for 30 minutes, stirring occasionally. Garnish with shredded cheese.

Serves 4

SPAGHETTI SOUP

MARGIE BUSH
PEORIA, IL

I love to make homemade soups in the winter for my family. Of all the soups I make, this is their favorite.

1 In a large skillet over medium heat, cook beef with onion, celery, green pepper, carrots and garlic until beef is browned and vegetables are tender. Drain; add water, sauce, tomatoes with juice and seasonings.

2 Increase heat to medium-high. Bring to a boil; stir in spaghetti. Cook for 10 to 15 minutes, stirring frequently, until spaghetti is tender.

Makes 10 servings

1 lb. lean ground beef
1 onion, chopped
2 stalks celery, diced
1 green pepper, diced
2 carrots, peeled and diced
2 cloves garlic, minced
5 to 6 c. water
15-oz. can spaghetti sauce
2 14-1/2 oz. cans diced tomatoes
1/2 t. Italian seasoning
1/2 t. salt
1/4 t. pepper
1/2 c. spaghetti, uncooked and broken into 2-inch pieces

EASY SLOW-COOKER BEEF STEW

CHRISTY NEUBERT
O'FALLON, IL

My sister, Crystal, gave me this wonderful recipe. It's so yummy and easy, all you need is fruit and warm bread to make a meal.

1 Place beef in bottom of a slow cooker sprayed with non-stick vegetable spray. Arrange carrots and potatoes over beef. Combine soups and pour over vegetables. Cover and cook on low setting for 8 to 10 hours or high setting for 6 hours.

Serves 3 to 4

1-1/2 lbs. stew beef cubes
8-oz. pkg. baby carrots
3 to 4 potatoes, cubed
10-3/4 oz. can tomato soup
10-3/4 oz. can beef broth
10-3/4 oz. can French onion soup

BECKIE'S GARLIC SOUP

BECKIE BUTCHER
ELGIN, IL

I invented this soup recipe on a cold Chicago afternoon. The last thing I wanted to do was leave the house, so I went through my refrigerator and my lazy Susan instead...this is the delicious result!

1/4 c. butter
3 cloves garlic, minced
1 onion, chopped
12-oz. can evaporated milk
14-1/2 oz. can chicken broth
2 T. grated Parmesan cheese
1-1/2 t. dried parsley
1/4 t. cayenne pepper

1 In a skillet over medium heat, melt butter; sauté garlic and onion until tender. Add remaining ingredients and bring to a boil.

2 Reduce heat and let simmer for 10 to 15 minutes, stirring occasionally.

Serves 4

ILLINOIS FUN FACT

Italian beef sandwiches are favorites in Illinois. Developed during the Depression in the 1920s and 1930s, the meat was roasted slowly to make it more tender and mixed with giardiniera (pickled vegetables) to enhance the flavor. Al's Italian Beef and Portillo's are favorite spots.

CAROL'S CREAMY TOMATO SOUP

**TORI WILLIS
CHAMPAIGN, IL**

*My Aunt Carol taught me the grilled-cheese crouton trick...
sometimes I use Cheddar cheese and wheat bread.*

1 In a stockpot over medium-low heat, simmer tomatoes and juice for 30 minutes. Purée tomato mixture and basil in a food processor; return to pot. Stir in remaining ingredients.

2 Cook over low heat, stirring until butter is melted; do not boil. Garnish with Grilled Cheese Croutons.

Serves 4

**4 tomatoes, peeled and
  diced
4 c. tomato juice
1/4 c. fresh basil
1 c. whipping cream
1/2 c. butter
salt and pepper to taste**

1 Combine butter and thyme; spread over one side of each bread slice. Place 3 slices in a skillet, buttered-side down. Top each with a cheese slice and a bread slice, buttered-side up. Cook over medium-high heat for 3 to 5 minutes per side, until toasted and golden. Cut into one-inch squares.

**GRILLED CHEESE
CROUTONS
1/4 c. butter, softened
1/4 t. dried thyme
6 slices bread
3 slices American
  cheese**

PARTY JOES

JULIE DAWSON
PROSPECT HEIGHTS, IL

A new twist on the classic Sloppy Joe. Super-simple to toss together and tasty too!

3 lbs. ground beef
2 c. onion, chopped
2 15-oz. cans tomato
   sauce
12-oz. jar chili sauce
1/2 c. steak sauce
1 T. garlic, chopped
10 to 12 onion sandwich
   rolls, split

1 Brown beef and onion in a skillet over medium heat; drain. Spoon beef mixture into a slow cooker. Stir sauces and garlic into beef mixture.

2 Cover and cook on low setting for 2 to 3 hours, until heated through. Serve on rolls for sandwiches.

Serves 10 to 12

STEAMBURGERS

ROBERTA OEST
ASTORIA, IL

My family & friends love this simple sandwich recipe. It's a perfect old-fashioned favorite paired with a chocolate cola or a root beer float!

2 lbs. ground beef chuck
2-1/4 T. onion soup mix
1 T. Worcestershire
   sauce
1/4 t. pepper
1/2 c. water
8 to 10 hamburger buns,
   split
Optional: catsup

1 Brown beef in a skillet over medium heat; drain. Spoon beef into a slow cooker; stir in soup mix, sauce, pepper and water.

2 Cover and cook on low setting for 2 to 4 hours, until heated through and liquid is absorbed. Spoon onto buns for sandwiches; top with catsup, if desired.

Serves 8 to 10

SHREDDED ITALIAN TURKEY

LANA RULEVISH
ASHLEY, IL

This is a deliciously different take on the shredded meat sandwich. Not only does it taste amazing, but it's a little better for you too.

1 Combine water and dressing mix in a slow cooker; stir to mix well. Add turkey and peppers plus juice to slow cooker. Cover and cook on low setting for 7 to 8 hours, until turkey is very tender.

2 Remove turkey from slow cooker; shred and return to juices in slow cooker. Serve shredded turkey on buns for sandwiches.

Serves 10 to 12

2 c. water

0.7-oz. pkg. Italian salad dressing mix

3 to 4-lb. boneless, skinless turkey breast

5 pepperoncini peppers, plus 2 T. juice

10 to 12 hamburger buns, split

BUFFALO CHICKEN SANDWICH

SUSAN BUETOW
DU QUOIN, IL

Besides looking tasty, this sandwich is very easy to make. It's my go-to recipe when hubby is having buddies over!

6 boneless chicken
  breasts
1 onion, chopped
6 stalks celery, chopped
2 to 3 T. olive oil
1/2 c. all-purpose flour
Optional: 1 t. seasoning
  salt
17-1/2 oz. bottle buffalo
  wing sauce
6 soft buns, split
Garnish: ranch or blue
  cheese salad dressing,
  crumbled blue cheese,
  additional wing sauce

1 Flatten chicken breasts to 1/4-inch thin between pieces of wax paper; set aside. In a skillet over medium-low heat, sauté onion and celery in oil until tender. In a shallow bowl, combine flour and seasoning salt, if using. Dredge chicken pieces in flour mixture.

2 Add chicken on top of onion mixture in pan. Cook for 5 minutes; flip chicken and cook an additional 5 minutes. Add buffalo wing sauce to pan. Cover; increase heat to medium, and cook 5 to 7 minutes, until chicken juices run clear. Serve on buns; garnish as desired.

Makes 6 sandwiches

HEARTY HAMBURGER STEW

JUDY PHELAN
MACOMB, IL

A comforting weeknight meal...and with just one pan, clean-up will be a breeze!

1 lb. ground beef
1 onion, chopped
1/2 c. celery, chopped
5-1/2 c. tomato juice
1 c. water
1/2 c. pearled barley,
  uncooked
2 t. chili powder
1 t. salt
1/2 t. pepper

1 In a large saucepan over medium heat, cook beef, onion and celery until beef is no longer pink. Drain; stir in remaining ingredients. Bring to a boil; reduce heat to low. Cover and simmer, stirring occasionally, for 50 minutes, or until barley is tender.

Makes 4 servings

CHRISTY'S TACO SOUP

CHRISTY WOOSLEY
BLOOMINGDALE, IL

This is an easy recipe to make either on the stovetop or in the slow cooker. Just brown, dump and warm...it's almost foolproof!

1 Brown beef in a soup pot over medium heat; drain. Add tomato sauce, undrained vegetables and taco seasoning. Bring to a boil; reduce heat to low. Cover and simmer at least 20 minutes, stirring occasionally. The longer the soup simmers, the better the flavor will be.

2 May also combine all ingredients except garnish in a slow cooker; cover and cook on low setting for 6 to 8 hours. Serve with crushed tortilla chips, cheese and a dollop of sour cream mixed into each bowl.

Serves 5

1 lb. ground beef
15-oz. can tomato sauce
15-1/2 oz. can kidney, pinto or Great Northern beans
14-1/2 oz. can diced tomatoes
15-oz. can sweet corn
1-1/4 oz. pkg. taco seasoning mix
Garnish: crushed tortilla chips, shredded Cheddar cheese, sour cream

BASIL-TOMATO GRILLED CHEESE

JO ANN
GOOSEBERRY PATCH

What's better than a grilled cheese sandwich? One that's chock-full of fresh ingredients from the farmers' market!

1 Top 4 slices of bread with 2 slices of mozzarella cheese each. Arrange tomato slices evenly over top. Drizzle with vinegar; sprinkle with basil, salt and pepper. Top with remaining bread slices; set aside. In a cup, combine oil, Parmesan cheese and garlic powder; brush over both sides of each sandwich.

2 Heat a large skillet or griddle over medium heat; add sandwiches. Cook until golden on both sides and cheese is melted.

Makes 4 sandwiches

8 slices Texas toast or other thick-sliced bread, divided
8 slices mozzarella cheese
2 to 3 roma tomatoes, sliced
2 t. balsamic vinegar
2 T. fresh basil, snipped
salt and pepper to taste
1/4 c. olive oil
3 T. shredded Parmesan cheese
1/4 t. garlic powder

HOAGIE DIP FOR SANDWICHES

PHYLLIS RACK
HOLLMAN ESTATES, IL

You'll be amazed how much this delicious spread tastes like a hoagie sandwich! This makes a lot, so feel free to halve the recipe. Sure to be a hit at parties.

1/2 lb. deli salami, diced
1/2 lb. deli boiled ham, diced
1/2 lb. American cheese, diced
1 c. lettuce, shredded
3/4 c. tomato, diced
1/4 c. onion, diced
1 c. mayonnaise
1 T. dried oregano
salt and pepper to taste
sliced Italian bread

1 In a large bowl, combine all ingredients except bread; mix well. Cover and keep refrigerated. If making ahead, add lettuce and tomato at serving time. Serve as a spread on slices of Italian bread.

Makes 12 servings

ILLINOIS FUN FACT

Chicago-style Vienna beef sandwiches...OK, hot dogs, have been a favorite for years, with their steamed poppy seed buns. Choose your toppings or let them be "dragged through the garden" with lots of toppings, such as chopped onions, green relish, tomato wedges, tiny sport peppers, dill pickle spears, mustard and absolutely NO catsup. There are various vendors, but they all start with the dogs.

HOT & COLD STROMBOLI

JESSICA BRANCH
COLCHESTER, IL

This is one of my hubby's favorites. I like it hot out of the oven and he likes it cold the day after. We munch on this for dinner, snacks or supper. It's also a tasty take-along treat...just pack it in a cooler.

1 Line a 15"x10" jelly-roll pan with parchment paper; spray with non-stick vegetable spray. Place both frozen loaves end-to-end on pan; thaw according to package directions. When thawed, roll out both loaves together to cover the pan.

2 Layer meats and cheese over dough; scatter green pepper, onion and olives over cheese. Sprinkle with seasonings. Roll up layered dough jelly-roll style; place seam-side down on pan. Let rise for one hour. Drizzle olive oil over rolled dough. Bake at 400 degrees for 15 minutes. Reduce oven temperature to 350 degrees; bake an additional 15 minutes. Slice and serve hot or cold.

Serves 8

2 loaves frozen bread dough
1/2 lb. deli ham, thinly sliced
1/2 lb. deli salami, thinly sliced
1/2 lb. deli bologna, thinly sliced
1/2 lb. Swiss cheese, thinly sliced
1/2 c. green pepper, diced
1/2 c. onion, diced
1/4 c. black olives, sliced
1/4 c. green olives, sliced
1/2 t. garlic salt
1/2 t. Italian seasoning
2 T. olive oil

OLD-TIME BEEF STEW

JAN SHERWOOD
CARPENTERSVILLE, IL

I have been making this stew since the mid-80s. I have such warm memories of sitting around the dinner table with my young family, enjoying this savory stew during blustery winter weather.

2 lbs. stew beef cubes

2 T. shortening

1 onion, sliced

4 c. tomato juice

1 T. lemon juice

1 T. sugar

1 T. Worcestershire sauce

1 T. salt

1 t. pepper

1 t. paprika

1/8 t. ground allspice or cloves

6 carrots, peeled and sliced

6 potatoes, peeled and cubed

1/2 c. cold water

1/4 c. all-purpose flour

1 In a Dutch oven over medium-high heat, brown beef cubes in shortening for 20 minutes. Drain; add onion, tomato juice, lemon juice, sugar, Worcestershire sauce and seasonings. Bring to a boil; reduce heat to medium-low.

2 Cover and simmer for 2 hours, stirring occasionally. Add carrots and potatoes; simmer 30 minutes longer, or until vegetables are tender. Combine water and flour in a cup; stir until smooth. Push beef and vegetables to one side of pan. Add flour mixture to pan; cook and stir until gravy is thickened.

Makes 8 servings

PRESSED PICNIC SANDWICH

JO ANN
GOOSEBERRY PATCH

Make this hearty sandwich ahead of time, then tuck it in the cooler when you're ready to head for the picnic grounds. Feel free to swap out your favorite deli meats, cheeses and toppings...you really can't go wrong with this recipe!

1 Slice loaf in half horizontally. Spread pesto over cut side of bottom half. Layer with salami, cheese, spinach or arugula and optional toppings, as desired. Season with salt and pepper.

2 Add top half of loaf. Wrap sandwich well with plastic wrap. Place sandwich on a plate; top with another plate and a cast-iron skillet or other heavy weight. Refrigerate for 6 hours to overnight. At serving time, unwrap sandwich; slice to serve.

Makes 8 servings

1 round loaf rustic
   bread
1/3 c. basil pesto sauce
1/2 lb. sliced deli salami
1/2 lb. sliced provolone
   cheese
1 c. fresh spinach or
   arugula, torn
Optional: roasted red
   peppers and/or chopped
   olive salad, well
   drained
salt and pepper to taste

CLASSIC CONEY SAUCE

SHERRY GORDON
ARLINGTON HEIGHTS, IL

Makes enough to satisfy a hungry team of Little Leaguers!

1 Combine all ingredients in a slow cooker. Cover and cook on high setting for 3 hours, stirring occasionally. Turn heat to low setting to keep warm.

Makes enough sauce for about 20 hot dogs

3 lbs. lean ground beef,
   browned and drained
28-oz. can tomato purée
1/2 c. onion, chopped
2 T. chili powder
1-1/2 T. mustard
1-1/2 T. Worcestershire
   saucee
1 t. garlic powder
salt and pepper to taste

RAPID REUBENS

DEB BLEAN
MORRISON, IL

Add some crisp dill pickles and crinkled potato chips...dinner is served!

12-oz. can corned beef, chopped
14-oz. pkg. sauerkraut, drained
8-oz. pkg. Swiss cheese slices
Thousand Island salad dressing to taste
8 slices rye bread, toasted

1 Place corned beef in a microwave-safe 2-quart casserole dish. Top with sauerkraut and cheese. Cover with plastic wrap.

2 Microwave on high for one to 2 minutes, or until cheese melts. Spread salad dressing on bread as desired. Top 4 bread slices with corned beef mixture; close with remaining bread.

Makes 4 sandwiches

CREAM OF ZUCCHINI SOUP

SUSAN MAURER
DAHLGREN, IL

One taste and you'll agree...there's really no such thing as too many zucchini!

3 lbs. zucchini, sliced 1/2-inch thick
2 onions, quartered
5 slices bacon
4 c. chicken broth
1 t. salt
1 t. pepper
Optional: 1/2 t. garlic powder
Garnish: onion and garlic croutons, or butter and grated Parmesan cheese

1 Combine all ingredients except garnish in a soup pot over medium heat. Cook until zucchini is tender and bacon is cooked, about 45 minutes. Ladle soup into a blender and process until smooth.

2 Return to soup pot; heat through. Serve topped with croutons or with a pat of butter and a sprinkling of Parmesan cheese.

Makes 6 servings

TORTELLINI & BROCCOLI SOUP

VICKY STANKUS
NEWTON, IL

A very tasty and filling soup that's perfect for warming the bones on a chilly day.

1 Add broth, water and lemon juice to a stockpot. Bring to a boil over medium-high heat. Add frozen tortellini and broccoli. Cook about 10 minutes, or until hot and tender.

Makes 4 servings

4 c. chicken broth
2 c. water
2 T. lemon juice
20-oz. pkg. frozen cheese tortellini, uncooked
1 c. frozen chopped broccoli

ELLA'S SAUERKRAUT SOUP

JAN SHERWOOD
CARPENTERSVILLE, IL

My sister Joanne shared this tasty recipe with me over 40 years ago, and I enjoy it just as much now as I did way back then! Sometimes I substitute crumbled crisp bacon or diced pork roast for the sausage.

1 Combine sauerkraut, broth and water in a large saucepan over medium heat. Cover; simmer for 30 minutes. Meanwhile, in a Dutch oven over medium heat, sauté onion in butter until translucent. Stir in flour and paprika; cook and stir for 3 minutes.

2 Add half of sauerkraut mixture to Dutch oven; stir until smooth. Add remaining sauerkraut mixture and potatoes. Reduce heat to low. Simmer for 30 minutes, stirring often. Add sausage and pepper; simmer for 10 more minutes.

Makes 6 servings

2 16-oz. pkgs. sauerkraut, drained and rinsed
6 c. low-sodium beef broth
2 c. water
1 c. onion, chopped
6 T. butter
1 c. all-purpose flour
1 t. paprika
2 potatoes, peeled and diced
1 lb. Kielbasa sausage, diced
pepper to taste

TRIPLE GARLIC STEAK SANDWICHES

ALICIA VAN DUYNE
BRAIDWOOD, IL

My husband and I both love garlic. We came up with this recipe one evening when we were experimenting with the grill. My children love these sandwiches, and I've had many requests to make them!

1 lb. sliced mushrooms

1 onion, thinly sliced

1 green pepper, thinly sliced

2 t. extra-virgin olive oil

2 t. garlic powder

6 thin-cut boneless beef ribeye steaks or sliced beef sandwich steaks

2 t. garlic salt

6 slices mozzarella cheese

1/2 c. butter, softened

3 T. garlic, pressed

6 hard rolls, split

Optional: favorite steak sauce

1 Place vegetables on a long piece of heavy-duty aluminum foil. Sprinkle with olive oil and garlic powder.

2 Place foil on grate over medium-high heat. Grill until vegetables are tender, about 10 to 12 minutes; remove from grill and set aside. Add steaks to grill and sprinkle with garlic salt. Cook to desired doneness, about 2 to 3 minutes per side.

3 Remove steaks from grill; top with cheese slices and keep warm. Blend butter and pressed garlic in a small bowl. Spread butter mixture over cut sides of rolls. Grill rolls cut-side down until toasted. To serve, top each roll with a steak, a spoonful of vegetable mixture and some steak sauce, if desired.

Serves 6

VEGETABLE CHEESE SOUP

TONI GROVES
BENLD, IL

I make this soup quite often. My sister shared the recipe with me...my family loves it!

1 In a soup pot over medium heat, cook bacon until partially crisp. Add sausage and onion; cook until sausage is browned. Drain; stir in remaining ingredients except cheese.

2 Simmer over medium-low heat until vegetables are tender, stirring occasionally, about 30 minutes. Remove from heat. Add cheese and stir until melted.

Makes 4 to 5 servings

3/4 lb. bacon, cut into 1-inch pieces

1/4 lb. ground Italian pork sausage

1/2 c. onion, chopped

3 c. beef broth

1/2 lb. sliced mushrooms

1/4 lb. carrots, peeled and sliced

2-1/2 stalks celery, diced

1/4 head cabbage, chopped

4 potatoes, peeled and sliced

1/8 t. cayenne pepper

3 slices pasteurized process cheese, 1/4 inch thick

WILLY STRANGE'S GOOD SOUP

JESSICA BRANCH
COLCHESTER, IL

*This recipe was given to me by my aunt. We were bored with chili...
we tried this flavor-filled soup and it immediately became a favorite!
Willy Strange was the name on the recipe and nobody knows why.
We still laugh about it because it is such a funny name for a soup.*

1 onion, diced
1 T. oil
1 lb. ground beef
2 10-3/4 oz. cans
  minestrone soup
10-3/4 oz. can tomato
  soup
15-oz. can ranch-style
  beans
10-oz. can diced
  tomatoes with green
  chiles
2 c. water
1/4 c. catsup
1/8 t. salt
1/8 t. pepper

1 In a Dutch oven over medium-high heat, sauté onion in oil. Add beef and brown; drain. Add remaining ingredients; bring to a boil. Reduce heat to low.

2 Cover and simmer for about 30 minutes, or until soup thickens.

Makes 8 servings

YIAYIA'S CHICKEN PITAS

TORI WILLIS
CHAMPAIGN, IL

Though not exactly like my grandma's famous Greek sandwiches, they're pretty darn close!

1 In a small bowl, stir together yogurt, cucumber, dill weed and mint; set aside. For each sandwich, layer a pita with lettuce, chicken, tomato and cheese.

2 Spoon yogurt mixture on top. Roll up pita and secure with a wooden toothpick. Serve immediately.

Makes 4 servings

1/2 c. plain yogurt
1/4 c. cucumber, finely chopped
1/2 t. dill weed
1/4 t. dried mint, crushed
4 pita bread rounds
4 lettuce leaves
2 c. cooked chicken, cubed
1 tomato, thinly sliced
1/3 c. crumbled feta cheese

SAUCY SLOW-COOKER PULLED PORK

KAREN CHRISTIANSEN
GLENVIEW, IL

I overheard part of this recipe while standing in the checkout line at the grocery store! I only knew some ingredients, so I came up with my own version.

1 Pat spice rub onto pork shoulder. Wrap pork in plastic wrap and refrigerate overnight. Add onions to a slow cooker and place unwrapped pork on top.

2 In a bowl, combine cranberry sauce and barbecue sauce. Pour sauce mixture over pork.

3 Cover and cook on low setting for 8 to 10 hours. Remove pork to a bowl and shred with 2 forks. Strain about 1-1/2 cups sauce from the slow cooker and stir into shredded pork. Serve on sandwich rolls.

Serves 6 to 8

1 T. barbecue spice rub
4-lb. boneless pork shoulder
1-1/2 yellow onions, sliced
2 16-oz. cans whole-berry cranberry sauce
18-oz. bottle barbecue sauce
6 to 8 sandwich rolls, split

ALL-AMERICAN SANDWICHES

**JO ANN
GOOSEBERRY PATCH**

*So simple to make yet so satisfying, these yummy turkey
sandwiches are aways a hit at our house!*

1-1/2 T. olive oil
1 red onion, thinly sliced
3-1/2 T. red wine
  vinegar
6 c. fresh arugula
  leaves, divided
1/4 c. mayonnaise
salt and pepper to taste
4 whole-grain small
  ciabatta rolls, halved
1/2 lb. thinly sliced
  smoked deli turkey
1/4 c. crumbled blue
  cheese

1 Heat oil in a skillet over medium-high heat.
Add onion and sauté until soft and lightly golden.
Remove from heat and stir in vinegar. Set aside.

2 Chop enough arugula to equal one cup. Stir in
mayonnaise; season with salt and pepper. Spread
arugula mixture over cut sides of rolls.

3 Divide turkey evenly among bottom halves of
rolls. Top with cheese, onion mixture, remaining
arugula leaves and top halves of rolls.

Serves 4

RASPBERRY-DIJON BAGUETTES

DEBORAH LOMAX
PEORIA, IL

A friend shared a similar recipe using roast beef...this is my spin on that recipe using grilled chicken.

1 Spread 4 slices of baguette with mustard. Top remaining slices with raspberry jam. Arrange a layer of grilled chicken over mustard; top with arugula and onion, if desired top with remaining baquette slices.

Serves 4

1 baguette, sliced
1 T. Dijon mustard
1 T. raspberry jam
4 boneless, skinless chicken breasts, grilled and sliced
2 c. arugula leaves
Optional: red onion slices

ILLINOIS FUN FACT

If you love gyros, you might want to look for Kronos Gyros, from Glendale Heights. Take your pick from lamb, beef or chicken cooked on a vertical cone, and served in a warm pita with veggies and tzatziki sauce.

CHAPTER FOUR

ALL-IN-THE-FAMILY

Mains

PULL UP A CHAIR AND GATHER

WITH FAMILY & FRIENDS TO

ENJOY A TASTY HOME-COOKED

DINNER USING FARM-FRESH

INGREDIENTS THAT ARE SURE

TO PLEASE.

BAKED SWEET-AND-SOUR CHICKEN

KRISTIN KNOWLES
DE SOTO, IL

While the ingredients may look odd at first...don't fret. All these flavors come together to create one mouthwatering meal! Plus, this dish is healthier than take-out since nothing's fried.

16-oz. jar French salad dressing

10-oz. jar peach or apricot preserves

1-1/2 oz. pkg. onion soup mix

1 T. water

3 to 4 boneless, skinless chicken breasts, cubed

3 c. long-cooking rice, uncooked

15-1/4 oz. can pineapple chunks, drained

1 to 2 green peppers, chopped

1 In a lightly greased 13"x9" baking pan, combine salad dressing, preserves, soup mix and water. Stir in chicken until evenly coated.

2 Bake, uncovered, at 350 degrees for 45 minutes, until chicken is no longer pink. Meanwhile, prepare rice according to package directions. Remove chicken from oven; stir in pineapple and green pepper. Bake for an additional 15 minutes. Serve over rice.

Makes 8 to 10 servings

FRIED CATFISH

DEBBIE NEMECEK
SPRINGFIELD, IL

Invite friends over for an old-fashioned fish fry! Kick up the flavor by adding the Cajun seasoning. Don't forget to include hushpuppies.

1 Soak fish in beer and baking soda one hour.

2 Combine milk, egg, salt, pepper and, if desired, Cajun seasoning. Drain fish and dip into milk mixture, then dredge in breading mix.

3 Pour oil to a depth of 2 inches in a large skillet. Heat to 375 degrees; fry fish, a few fillets at a time, until golden.

Serves 5

3 lbs. catfish fillets
12-oz. can beer
2 T. baking soda
2 c. milk
1 egg
1 T. salt
1 T. pepper
Optional: 2 T. Cajun seasoning
8-oz. pkg. fish breading mix
oil for frying

ILLINOIS FUN FACT

There's a fishing industry in the state, mostly from inland rivers, such as the Illinois and Mississippi. Main catches include catfish, carp, sturgeon, and buffalo fish. Most of the rest are taken from Lake Michigan, including smelt, yellow perch and chubs.

CHICKEN NOODLE CASSEROLE

MARY BETH UPDIKE
OTTAWA, IL

My mom created this recipe and it is a favorite of mine. Nothing turns a day around quicker than coming home to this dish!

2 T. butter

2 T. all-purpose flour

1 t. chicken bouillon granules

1 c. boiling water

10-3/4 oz. can cream of chicken soup

1-1/2 c. cooked chicken, diced

8-oz. pkg. wide egg noodles, cooked

1 c. potato chips, crushed

1 Melt butter in a large saucepan over medium heat; stir in flour. Dissolve bouillon in boiling water; add to pan.

2 Stir in soup and chicken; heat through. Add noodles; pour into a greased 2-quart casserole dish. Sprinkle with crushed chips. Bake, uncovered, at 325 degrees for 15 minutes.

Makes 4 servings

HEARTY CHICKEN BOG

NICOLE MANLEY
GREAT LAKES, IL

When I was little, I used to go to South Carolina to visit my grandparents for the summer. One year they took me to a town festival featuring this delicious local specialty. Recently I had a craving and decided to try to recreate it my own way...I think I've gotten it pretty close!

1 Melt butter in a large stockpot over medium heat. Add onion, carrots and celery; sauté for 2 minutes. Add sausage and chicken; stir. Add water and seasonings; bring to a slow boil.

2 Cover and simmer for 45 minutes. When chicken juices run clear, remove from pot; set aside to cool for a few minutes.

3 Stir in rice; cover and cook over low heat for 10 minutes. Pull chicken from bone; return chicken to stockpot and stir well. Discard bay leaves before serving.

Serves 6

1/2 c. butter
1 c. onion, chopped
2 carrots, peeled and diced
2 stalks celery, diced
1 lb. smoked pork sausage, cut in 1-inch pieces
3 lbs. chicken thighs
8 c. water
2 t. Cajun seasoning
2 t. seasoning salt
2 bay leaves
salt and pepper to taste
4 c. instant rice, uncooked

EASY CHICKEN & NOODLES

RAMONA STORM
GARDNER, IL

This smells so good and warms you up on a cold day. Leftover cooked chicken works great. Add some warm, crusty bread and a citrus salad...dinner is served!

16-oz. pkg. frozen egg noodles, uncooked

2 14-1/2 oz. cans chicken broth

2 10-3/4 oz. cans cream of chicken soup

1/2 c. onion, finely chopped

1/2 c. carrot, peeled and diced

1/2 c. celery, diced

salt and pepper to taste

2 c. boneless, skinless chicken breasts, cooked and cubed

1 Thaw egg noodles (or run package under warm water) just enough to break apart; set aside.

2 Spray a slow cooker with non-stick vegetable spray. Add remaining ingredients except chicken; blend well. Stir in noodles and chicken. Cover and cook on low setting for 7 to 8 hours, until hot and bubbly.

Makes 8 servings

GRANDMA'S CHICKEN NO-PEEK

KRISTEN LEWIS
BOURBONNAIS, IL

This is one of my grandma's favorite recipes. It's such a satisfying dish that will always remind me of her.

1 Spread uncooked rice and seasoning mix in the bottom of a greased 13"x9" baking pan. Combine canned soups and water in a bowl; pour over rice. Place chicken on top; sprinkle with soup mix.

2 Cover tightly and bake at 350 degrees for 2-1/2 hours. Do not peek!

Makes 4 servings

6-oz. pkg. long-grain and wild rice mix, uncooked

10-3/4 oz. can cream of mushroom soup

10-3/4 oz. can cream of celery soup

1 c. water

4 chicken breasts

1.35-oz. pkg. onion soup mix

ILLINOIS FUN FACT

Saganaki, a Greek specialty featuring flaming cheese, with brandy poured over it at tableside in restaurants, has become popular at many restaurants in Illinois. The cheese gets crispy on the outside. Everyone yells "Opa." Different restaurants specialize in using different cheeses.

MEDITERRANEAN HERB RUB

**TORI WILLIS
CHAMPAIGN, IL**

This flavorful rub works wonders on grilled chicken or beef.

1/3 c. grated Parmesan
 cheese
1/3 c. pepper
2 T. dried thyme
2 T. dried rosemary
2 T. dried basil
1 t. garlic powder
1 t. salt

1 Mix together cheese and pepper; add remaining ingredients and stir well. If a finer texture is desired, process in a food processor. Store in an airtight container up to one week. To use, rub over chicken or beef; grill as desired.

Makes one cup

SOUR CREAM CHILI BAKE

**VICTORIA WRIGHT
ORLAND PARK, IL**

My mom shared this recipe with me when I was a teenager. I don't know if it was her own creation or not, but she made it her own! Whenever I make this dish I'm reminded of both my mom and of Arizona...I miss them both very much!

1 lb. ground turkey or
 beef
15-oz. can chili beans,
 drained
10-oz. can hot enchilada
 sauce
8-oz. can tomato sauce
1 T. dried, minced onion
1-1/2 c. shredded
 American cheese,
 divided
2 c. tortilla chips,
 coarsely crushed and
 divided
1 c. sour cream

1 In a large skillet over medium heat, brown meat; drain. Stir in beans, sauces, onion and one cup cheese; mix well. Stir in one cup crushed tortilla chips. Transfer to a greased 1-1/2 quart casserole dish.

2 Cover and bake at 375 degrees for 30 minutes. Sprinkle remaining chips around edge of casserole. Spoon sour cream evenly over top; sprinkle with remaining cheese. Bake, uncovered, until cheese melts, about 5 to 10 minutes.

Serves 6

NANNY'S FAMOUS BEEF STROGANOFF

SANDY LAKEMAN
ALGONQUIN, IL

Saucy beef and noodles...so good on a chilly day!

1 In a large skillet over medium heat, sauté mushrooms and onion in 2 tablespoons butter. Remove mixture to a bowl and set aside.

2 Toss beef in flour, coating thoroughly. Add remaining butter to skillet and brown beef; add broth, water and salt. Reduce heat. Cover and simmer until beef is tender, stirring occasionally, about 1-1/2 hours. Add mushroom mixture and sour cream; heat through. Serve over cooked noodles.

Serves 6

1/2 lb. sliced mushrooms
1 onion, chopped
1/4 c. butter, divided
2 lbs. beef round steak, cut into 2-1/2 inch strips
1/4 to 1/2 c. all-purpose flour
10-1/2 oz. can beef broth
3/4 c. water
1 t. salt
8-oz. container sour cream
cooked egg noodles

ANTIPASTO-STYLE LINGUINE

VICKIE
GOOSEBERRY PATCH

I've always been a big fan of antipasto. I love having all the same flavors over pasta.

12-oz. pkg. linguine pasta, uncooked

16-oz. jar antipasto salad with olives, divided

3 T. olive oil

4 portabella mushroom caps, sliced

6-oz. pkg. sliced deli salami, cut into thin strips

2 c. shredded Asiago cheese, divided

2 c. fresh basil, chopped and divided

pepper to taste

1 Cook pasta and drain, reserving 1/2 cup cooking water; set aside. Measure one cup antipasto salad vegetables and 6 tablespoons marinade from jar; reserve remainder for another recipe. Slice vegetables and set aside.

2 Heat oil in pasta pot over medium-high heat. Sauté mushrooms until tender, about 6 minutes. Add salami; cook and stir briefly. Add pasta, reserved cooking water, vegetables, reserved marinade and 1-1/2 cups cheese; toss until liquid thickens and coats pasta, about 3 minutes. Stir in 1-1/2 cups basil; add pepper to taste. Garnish with remaining basil and cheese.

Serves 4 to 6

KITCHEN TIP

Add some fresh broccoli or snow peas to a favorite pasta recipe. Simply drop chopped veggies into the pasta pot about halfway through the cooking time. Pasta and veggies will be tender at about the same time.

GRANDMA B'S PIG IN A BLANKET

KRYSTAL HENRY
NASHVILLE, IL

This is one of my favorite comfort foods of all time...an easy take on stuffed cabbage rolls that makes the house smell delicious. Going to Grandma's farm on the weekends was always my favorite thing to do...fishing, climbing trees, picking veggies from the garden, and just running around in the fresh country air, followed by a wonderful meal cooked by Grandma.

1 In a skillet over medium heat, brown beef with onion, garlic, salt and pepper. Drain and set aside. Combine undrained tomatoes and rice. Add beef mixture and mix well; transfer to a greased 13"x9" baking pan. Place shredded cabbage on top. Drizzle one cup of tomato juice over cabbage.

2 Bake, uncovered, at 350 degrees for 20 minutes; add remaining tomato juice if needed. Cover with aluminum foil. Bake an additional hour, or until rice and cabbage are tender.

Serves 6 to 8

1-1/2 lbs. ground beef
1 onion, diced
2 cloves garlic, diced
salt and pepper to taste
2 28-oz. cans diced tomatoes
1 c. instant rice, uncooked
1 head cabbage, shredded
2 c. tomato juice, divided

JENNIFER'S CHICKEN STUFF

JENNIFER SIEVERS
CAROL STREAM, IL

The first time I made this hearty dish for dinner, it was a hit with both my daughters. A week later, the younger one asked me to make "that chicken stuff" again and the name just stuck!

1 onion, diced

2 carrots, peeled and diced

2 stalks celery, diced

6 boneless, skinless chicken breasts

2 c. brown rice, uncooked

32-oz. container chicken broth

salt and pepper to taste

1 In a slow cooker, layer all ingredients except salt and pepper in order listed.

2 Cover and cook on low setting for about 8 hours, until chicken is very tender. Stir well to break up chicken and mix everything together. Season with salt and pepper to taste

Serves 6

KITCHEN TIP

The secret to tender steamed rice! Cook long-cooking rice according to package directions. When it's done, remove pan from heat, cover with a folded tea towel and put lid back on. Let stand for 5 to 10 minutes before serving.

Chili-Weather Chili, p48

Whether you are looking for a quick-to-make breakfast dish to start the day off right, no-fuss party fare for those special guests, satisfying soups and sandwiches for the perfect lunch, main dishes to bring them to the table fast, or a sweet little something to savor at the end of the meal, you'll love these recipes from the amazing cooks in beautiful Illinois.

Apple Wheels, p25

Cream of Zucchini Soup, p60

Peachy Waffle Topping, p14

Peanut Butter Surprise Cookies, p134

Buffalo Chicken Sandwich, p54

Peanut Butter-Honey Spread, p119

Autumn Apple Milkshake, p142

Chicken Salad Croissants, p44

Carol's Creamy Tomato Soup, p51

Peppermint Bark Brownies, p147

Fried Catfish, p71

Bacon Griddle Cakes, p16

Joyce's Chocolate Chip Pie, p129

Chicken-Salsa Dip, p121

Antipasto-Style Linguine, p78

Black Bean Breakfast Burritos, p8

Pineapple-Nut Cookies, p131

Yiayia's Chicken Pitas, p65

Quick & Easy Parmesan Asparagus, p37

Good Morning Blueberry Shake, p112

Mini Turkey-Berry Bites, p118

Minted Baby Carrots, p34

Oatmeal-Carrot Cookies, p133

Ripe Tomato Tart, p38

Pumpkin Pie Pudding, p142

Pepperoni Pizza Rigatoni, p93

Easy Chicken & Noodles, p74

Chicago Italian Beef, p42

Rosemary-Dijon Chicken Croissants, p45

Saucy Slow-Cooker Pulled Pork, p65

Sugarplum Bacon, p19

Summer in a Bowl, p25

Classic Coney Sauce, p59

Zippy Broiled Catfish, p91

MEGGIE'S RATATOUILLE

TORI WILLIS
CHAMPAIGN, IL

When my friend Meggie served this dish at a harvest get-together, I couldn't get enough. I had to have the recipe before I left!

1 Sauté vegetables with salad dressing in a large oven-proof skillet over medium heat. Add tomatoes with juice; cook for 15 minutes. Sprinkle with cheeses.

2 Bake, uncovered, at 350 degrees for 15 minutes.

Serves 6 to 8

1 eggplant, peeled and cut into 1-inch cubes

1 onion, diced

1 red pepper, diced

1 zucchini, cut into 1-inch cubes

1/4 c. sun-dried tomato salad dressing

14-1/2 oz. can diced tomatoes

1/4 c. grated Parmesan cheese

1 c. shredded mozzarella cheese

SAVORY SALISBURY STEAK

DEE DEE PLZAK
WESTMONT, IL

My mother shared this recipe with me. For some reason, my kids like it better when Grandma cooks it and always ask for "her" Salisbury steak instead of mine...it must be the dish she serves it in!

1 In a small bowl, mix 3/4 cup soup and water; set aside. In a separate bowl, mix remaining soup and other ingredients.

2 Form into small patties; arrange in a single layer in a greased 13"x9" baking pan. Bake, uncovered, at 350 degrees for 30 minutes. Drain; spoon reserved soup mixture over patties. Bake, uncovered, an additional 10 to 12 minutes.

Serves 4 to 6

10-3/4 oz. can golden mushroom soup, divided

1/3 c. water

1-1/2 lbs. lean ground beef

1 onion, finely chopped

1/2 c. bread crumbs

1 egg, beaten

1/2 t. salt

1/8 t. pepper

BIG BUTTERFLIES & MUSHROOMS

**ISOLDA CROCKETT
MOSSVILLE, IL**

I'm half Italian, and my fondest memories are of sitting in Nana's big kitchen while she cooked and talked to me.

1/2 c. butter
5 shallots, chopped
1-1/2 lbs. mushrooms, chopped
1/2 c. chicken broth
1/2 t. salt
1/4 t. cayenne pepper
16-oz. pkg. large bowtie pasta, cooked
1/2 c. grated Romano cheese

1 Melt butter in a skillet over medium heat. Add shallots and cook until soft. Add mushrooms and broth to skillet. Lower heat and simmer for 4 to 5 minutes, stirring often. Add seasonings; stir well and cook for 5 more minutes.

2 Place cooked pasta in a warmed large serving bowl; add cheese and toss. Pour mushroom sauce over pasta and gently toss to coat well. Serve warm or chilled.

Makes 6 servings

PORK & PEACH KABOBS

**ED SMULSKI
LYONS, IL**

Ripe nectarines and pineapple are luscious with pork too.

2 peaches, halved, pitted and cut into 6 wedges
1 sweet onion, cut into 6 wedges
1-1/2 lbs. pork tenderloin, cut into 18 to 20 cubes
6 skewers
3/4 c. honey barbecue sauce
Optional: cooked brown rice

1 Cut peach and onion wedges crosswise in half. Thread peach, onion and pork pieces alternately onto skewers, leaving some space in between for even grilling.

2 Grill skewers over medium-high heat for 15 minutes or until pork juices run clear, turning skewers occasionally. Brush with barbecue sauce during the last 5 minutes. Serve with cooked rice, if desired.

Makes 6 servings

PENNY-PINCHING PORK

**LOIS EDBERG
DOWNERS GROVE, IL**

When dollars and time are tight, this is my go-to recipe. Plus, I usually always have the ingredients to make it in my cupboard. The caraway seed adds amazing flavor to this roast.

1 Place sauerkraut in a slow cooker. Top with sliced potatoes and onion; set aside. In a bowl, mix together flour, seasonings and raisins; sprinkle over potatoes and onions. Place roast on top of seasonings.

2 Cover and cook on low setting for 4 to 6 hours, until roast is no longer pink in the center.

Serves 4

27-oz. can sauerkraut, drained
3 potatoes, peeled and sliced
1 onion, sliced
3 T. all-purpose flour
1 t. caraway seed
1 t. paprika
pepper to taste
1/3 c. raisins
1-1/2 lb. pork butt roast

ZIPPY BROILED CATFISH

**MARDELL ROSS
GENOA, IL**

Pop this in the oven and by the time you toss the salad and set the table, dinner is served!

1 Brush fillets with lemon juice; sprinkle with salt and pepper. Dredge fillets in flour. Arrange on a well-greased broiler pan; brush with salad dressing.

2 Broil about 4 inches from heat source for 4 to 6 minutes, basting occasionally with salad dressing. Turn carefully; brush with additional salad dressing. Broil for an additional 4 to 6 minutes, until fish flakes easily.

Serves 6

6 catfish fillets
1/4 c. lemon juice
1 t. salt
1/8 t. pepper
1 c. all-purpose flour
1-1/3 c. Italian salad dressing

MUSHROOM CHICKEN

KATHY RIGG
MOUNT STERLING, IL

This is my go-to recipe. The mushrooms add such a rich flavor and it is a good looking dinner as well. Add a crisp salad or a steamed veggie and dinner is ready.

Optional: 1 T. oil

4 boneless, skinless chicken breasts

8-oz. pkg. white mushrooms, quartered

6-oz. pkg. shiitake mushrooms, stems removed and caps sliced

1/4 c. butter

0.7-oz. pkg. Italian salad dressing mix

10-3/4 oz. can golden mushroom soup

1/2 c. cream cheese

2 T. fresh chives, snipped

2 T. dried, minced onion

1/2 c. dry white wine or chicken broth

cooked angel hair pasta

Optional: chopped green onions

1 If desired, heat oil in a large skillet over medium heat; brown chicken on both sides. (Browning step may be omitted.)

2 Combine mushrooms in a 4-quart slow cooker; top with chicken and set aside. Melt butter in a saucepan over medium heat; stir in dressing mix. Add soup, cream cheese, chives, onion and wine or broth; stir until cream cheese is melted. Spoon mixture over chicken.

3 Cover and cook on low setting for 4 to 5 hours, until chicken juices run clear. Serve chicken and sauce over cooked pasta. If desired, sprinkle with green onions.

Makes 4 servings

PEPPERONI-PIZZA RIGATONI

JO ANN
GOOSEBERRY PATCH

Personalize this recipe by adding mushrooms, black olives or any of your family's other favorite pizza toppings.

1 Alternate layers of ground beef, cooked rigatoni, cheese, soup, sauce and pepperoni in a slow cooker.

2 Cover and cook on low setting for 4 hours.

Makes 6 servings

1-1/2 lbs. ground beef, browned and drained

8-oz. pkg. rigatoni pasta, cooked

16-oz. pkg. shredded mozzarella cheese

10-3/4 oz. can tomato soup

2 14-oz. jars pizza sauce

8-oz. pkg. sliced pepperoni

PORK TENDERLOIN TOWERS

PEARL TEISERSKAS
BROOKFIELD, IL

I received this delicious recipe from a dear friend of mine back in 1951. She passed away in 2004, but each time I make this dish I still think about her.

1 Season patties with salt and pepper. Place in a lightly greased 13"x9" baking pan. Top each patty with a slice of onion, tomato and cheese. Criss-cross 2 half-slices of bacon on top of each patty; use a wooden toothpick to hold in place.

2 Bake, covered, at 350 degrees for one hour. Uncover and bake for 15 minutes longer, or until pork is tender and bacon is crisp.

Makes 6 servings

6 pork tenderloin patties or pork cutlets

1 t. salt

1/4 t. pepper

6 thin slices onion

6 slices tomato

6 slices sharp Cheddar cheese

6 slices bacon, cut in half

TURKEY-SAUSAGE MEATLOAF

**PEARL TEISERSKAS
BROOKFIELD, IL**

My family & friends always request this meatloaf when I bring it to our church socials. The recipe was handed down from my grandmother, who was a wonderful cook. It is not only easy to make, but delicious and filled with good-for-you ingredients.

1-1/2 lbs. ground turkey
1 lb. ground pork sausage
10-oz. pkg. frozen spinach, thawed and squeezed dry
1 onion, chopped
2 to 3 carrots, peeled and chopped
1 clove garlic, chopped
1 t. dried thyme
1 t. dried marjoram
1 t. salt
3/4 t. pepper
1/2 c. dry bread crumbs
2 eggs, beaten

1 In a large bowl, combine all ingredients except bread crumbs and eggs; mix well. Add bread crumbs and eggs; mix thoroughly.

2 Pack mixture loosely into a lightly greased 9"x5" loaf pan, rounding top slightly. Bake at 350 degrees for about one hour and 15 minutes, until a meat thermometer reads 160 degrees when inserted in center of meatloaf. Drain any fat; turn meatloaf onto a cutting board. Slice into thick slices. Serve hot or cold.

Makes 8 servings

PORK CHOP DELIGHT

JANET VAUGHN
DARIEN, IL

This is a recipe passed down from my mother. She was a great cook though she didn't even like to cook! This recipe is still a favorite all these years later. They literally melt in your mouth...thanks, Mom!

1 Place pork chops in an ungreased 13"x9" baking pan. Add water to bottom of pan to prevent sticking. Top each pork chop with a tablespoon of chili sauce; sprinkle brown sugar over all.

2 Bake, uncovered, at 325 degrees for one hour; do not turn pork chops over.

Makes 8 servings

8 boneless thin-sliced pork chops
1/3 c. water
1/2 c. chili sauce, divided
1-1/2 c. brown sugar, packed

ILLINOIS FUN FACT

A favorite of many in Illinois, the Horseshoe Sandwich features an open-faced beef patty, slathered in French fries, and topped with melted cheese sauce.

SAUCY PORK, PEPPERS & PASTA

VICKIE
GOOSEBERRY PATCH

A wonderful one-skillet meal that's out of the ordinary! Sometimes I'll jazz it up with curly cavatappi pasta.

12-oz. pkg. penne pasta, uncooked
2 T. olive oil, divided
1 green pepper, cut into strips
1 red pepper, cut into strips
1 onion, cut into wedges
4 center-cut pork chops
salt and pepper to taste
1/2 c. all-purpose flour
26-oz. jar tomato & roasted garlic pasta sauce
1/2 c. white wine or chicken broth
1/2 t. dried thyme

1 Cook pasta according to package directions; drain. Meanwhile, heat one tablespoon oil in a large skillet over medium-high heat. Cook peppers and onion until crisp-tender. Remove vegetables to a bowl and set aside. Season pork chops lightly with salt and pepper; coat with flour. Add remaining oil to skillet; brown pork chops on both sides.

2 Reduce heat to low; stir in pasta sauce, wine or broth and thyme. Cover and simmer for 30 minutes, stirring occasionally, or until pork chops are tender. Remove pork chops to a plate. Stir vegetable mixture into sauce mixture and heat through. Serve pork chops and sauce over cooked pasta.

Makes 4 servings

PORK IN MUSTARD SAUCE

LYNDA BOLTON
EAST PEORIA, IL

When our kids were home, I was all about quick & easy skillet meals, and this one was a favorite! I love it because I usually have most of the necessary ingredients on hand.

1 Heat oil in a large skillet over medium heat. Brown pork chops on both sides; drain. Meanwhile, place carrots in a microwave-safe bowl; add enough water to cover. Microwave for 2-1/2 to 3 minutes; drain and set aside.

2 Pour chicken broth over pork chops in skillet; season with salt and pepper. Bring to a boil over medium-high heat. Add carrots and mushrooms to skillet; reduce heat to low. Cover and simmer until pork chops are tender, 30 to 40 minutes. Remove pork chops to a platter and cover to keep warm, reserving cooking juices in skillet.

3 In a small bowl, combine mustard, water and flour; mix well. Pour mustard mixture into reserved juices in skillet. Cook and stir over medium heat for one to 2 minutes, until thickened. To serve, spoon thickened sauce over pork chops and cooked rice or noodles, if desired.

Makes 4 to 6 servings

2 T. oil

4 to 6 bone-in or boneless pork chops

1 c. carrots, peeled and sliced

1 c. chicken broth

salt and pepper to taste

1 lb. sliced mushrooms

1/4 c. mustard

1/4 c. water

2 T. all-purpose flour

Optional: cooked rice or egg noodles

TOSTADA PIZZA

**KARA GUILLIAMS
CREVE COEUR, IL**

A Mexican twist on an Italian dish! Spice it up by adding some crushed red pepper flakes or fresh diced jalapeño pepper...make it even tastier by using queso fresco instead of Cheddar cheese.

1 lb. ground beef

1-1/4 oz. pkg. taco seasoning mix

1 t. chili powder

4-oz. can diced green chiles, drained

3/4 c. water

1 T. cornmeal

10-oz. tube refrigerated pizza dough

16-oz. can refried beans with chiles

8-oz. bottle taco sauce

1 c. shredded Cheddar cheese

1 c. shredded lettuce

1 tomato, chopped

1/2 c. green onions, sliced

1 Brown beef in a skillet over medium heat; drain. Add taco seasoning, chili powder, chiles and water to beef. Bring to a boil; reduce heat and simmer for 20 minutes, or until liquid is evaporated. Meanwhile, sprinkle cornmeal in a lightly greased 13"x9" baking pan. Roll pizza dough into a 12-inch by 8-inch rectangle; place in pan.

2 Bake at 400 degrees for 5 minutes. Spread refried beans evenly over baked crust. Pour taco sauce over beans; spoon beef mixture over sauce. Bake for 10 minutes, until crust is golden. Sprinkle with cheese; bake for an additional 2 minutes, or until cheese is melted. Top with lettuce, tomato and onions before serving.

Serves 6

SLOW-COOKED PIEROGIES

SHERRY GORDON
ARLINGTON HEIGHTS, IL

These buttery pierogies are yummy with a steamed green veggie. Frozen pierogies come in lots of different flavors...I keep several tucked in the freezer to go with whatever else is on the menu.

1 Place frozen pierogies in a lightly greased slow cooker; set aside. Melt butter in a skillet over medium heat; cook onion until golden.

2 Spoon mixture over pierogies; add salt and pepper to taste. Cover and cook on high setting for 3 hours. Turn pierogies with tongs twice during cooking time to coat with butter mixture.

Serves 8

2 16-oz. pkgs. frozen
  potato and cheese
  pierogies, uncooked
1/2 c. butter, sliced
1/2 to 1 onion, chopped
salt and pepper to taste

ILLINOIS FUN FACT

Eastern Europe pierogies have found fans in Illinois. Little dough pillows, akin to ravioli, are filled with meat, potatoes or cheese and boiled in water to cook.

TURKEY & POTATO HAND PIES

VICKIE
GOOSEBERRY PATCH

These little hand pies are perfect for parties or gatherings...no plates, no mess!

2 T. olive oil
1 onion, finely chopped
salt and pepper to taste
1 russet potato, peeled and diced
1 t. curry powder
3/4 c. peas
1/4 c. golden raisins, chopped
1 T. red wine vinegar
1-1/2 c. cooked turkey, shredded
2 9-inch pie crusts
1 egg, beaten

1 Heat oil in a large skillet over medium heat. Add onion, salt and pepper to oil. Cover and cook, stirring occasionally, for 4 minutes. Add potato to skillet and cook, covered, stirring occasionally until potato is tender, about 6 to 7 minutes. Stir in curry powder; remove from heat. Add peas, raisins and vinegar; mix to combine. Fold in turkey.

2 Cut each pie crust into 4 triangles. Divide turkey mixture evenly among triangles. Fold dough over filling, pressing seams together with a fork to seal. Place hand pies on a baking sheet and brush with beaten egg. Bake at 400 degrees for 15 to 20 minutes, until golden.

Serves 4

YUMMY MEATBALL SKEWERS

SHERRY GORDON
ARLINGTON HEIGHTS, IL

My kids love these skewers! What's more fun than dinner on a stick? Sometimes we add cherry tomatoes and zucchini chunks too.

1 Place 3 meatballs on each skewer, alternating with pepper, pineapple and onion pieces. Place skewers on a grill over medium heat.

2 Cook for 10 to 12 minutes, turning skewers occasionally. Brush with sauce during last 5 minutes of grilling.

Serves 8 to 10

28-oz. pkg. frozen
  meatballs, thawed
2 green and/or red
  peppers, cut into 1-inch
  squares
2 c. pineapple cubes
1 red onion, cut into
  1-inch squares
1-1/2 c. teriyaki sauce
8 to 10 skewers

GARLIC FRENCH BREAD

BRITTANY COWAN
BEARDSTOWN, IL

This is a great, easy side that can go with about any meal!

1 In a bowl, stir together melted butter and seasonings. Brush butter mixture over both sides of each bread slice.

2 Reassemble loaf on a piece of aluminum foil; wrap well. Place on a baking sheet. Bake at 350 degrees for 15 to 20 minutes, until bread starts to brown on the bottom.

Makes 8 to 10 servings

3/4 c. butter, melted
1/4 t. onion powder
1/4 t. garlic salt
1 loaf French bread,
  sliced

CABBAGE CRESCENT ROLLS

LANA RULEVISH
ASHLEY, IL

I have had this recipe for years. It's much quicker to fix than traditional cabbage rolls with the beef mixture rolled up in cabbage leaves. Many of my guests have said they like it better too!

1 lb. lean ground beef
1 head cabbage, finely chopped
1/4 c. water
1/8 t. garlic salt
salt and pepper to taste
8-oz. tube refrigerated crescent rolls
Optional: melted butter
1 c. shredded Cheddar cheese

1 In a large skillet over medium heat, brown beef; drain. Add cabbage, water and seasonings; stir thoroughly. Cover and simmer for about 15 minutes.

2 Press crescent rolls together in pairs to form rectangles; place on a lightly greased baking sheet. Spoon meat mixture onto rolls. Fold 2 opposite corners to the center; use a fork to crimp edges and pierce top. Bake at 350 degrees for 10 minutes, or until golden. Remove from oven; brush tops with butter, if desired. Sprinkle with cheese; serve immediately.

Makes 4 servings

CABBAGE PATCH

JENNIFER CRISP
ABINGDON, IL

Old-fashioned comfort food at its best, and this recipe feeds a crowd! Leftovers, if you have any, freeze wonderfully.

1 In a skillet over medium heat, brown beef and onion; drain. Add beef mixture to a slow cooker; add tomatoes with juice and remaining ingredients. Mix well.

2 Cover and cook on low setting for 4 to 5 hours, until vegetables are soft.

Serves 10

1-1/2 lbs. ground beef
1 onion, diced
2 14-1/2 oz. cans diced tomatoes
2 15-oz. cans kidney beans, drained and rinsed
2 14-oz. cans beef broth
3 stalks celery, diced
3 potatoes, peeled and diced
4 carrots, peeled and diced
1 head cabbage, chopped
1 T. sugar
ground cumin, garlic powder, pepper and onion salt to taste

CHICKEN OREGANO

JULIE BRUNINGA
EDWARDSVILLE, IL

Serve over thin spaghetti...pass the Parmesan cheese, please!

1-1/2 lbs. boneless,
  skinless chicken
  breasts
15-oz. can tomato sauce
28-oz. can diced
  tomatoes
1 green pepper, thinly
  sliced
1 onion, thinly sliced
1 t. garlic salt
1 t. dried oregano
salt and pepper to taste
1/2 c. shredded
  mozzarella cheese

1 Place chicken in a lightly greased 13"x9" baking pan. Top with sauce and tomatoes. Arrange green pepper and onion on top; sprinkle with seasonings and cheese.

2 Bake, uncovered, at 375 degrees for 30 minutes, until chicken juices run clear.

Serves 4

GARLIC BUBBLE BREAD

JOANNE GROSSKOPF
LAKE IN THE HILLS, IL

We love to serve this with spaghetti and a nice green salad.

16-oz. frozen bread
  dough, thawed
1/4 c. butter, melted
1 T. dried parsley
1 t. garlic powder
1/2 t. garlic salt
Optional: sesame or
  poppy seed

1 Cut dough into one-inch pieces. Combine butter, parsley, garlic power and garlic salt in a small bowl. Dip dough pieces into butter mixture to coat; layer in a buttered 9"x5" loaf pan. Sprinkle sesame or poppy seed over top, if desired. Cover dough with plastic wrap; let rise in a warm place (85 degrees), free from drafts, about one hour, until double in bulk.

2 Bake at 350 degrees for 30 minutes, or until golden. Cool completely in pan on a wire rack.

Serves 4 to 6

CHICKEN POT PIE

KATE KELLY GALLEGOS
AURORA, IL

My son, Frankie, loves to help make this for dinner.

1 Mix together chicken, soup, vegetables and celery. Spoon into a lightly greased 9"x9" baking pan. Separate and flatten rolls; place on top of mixture.

2 Bake for 25 minutes at 350 degrees, or until bubbly and rolls are golden.

Serves 4

2 to 3-lb. deli roast chicken, shredded or chopped

10-3/4 oz. can cream of mushroom soup with roasted garlic

16-oz. pkg. frozen mixed vegetables, thawed

2 stalks celery, chopped

12-oz. tube refrigerated dinner rolls

MOTHER'S SAUSAGE SUPPER

RACHEL BURCH
ILLIOPOLIS, IL

My mom was a nurse and she would toss this in the slow cooker before leaving for work. When my sister Elizabeth and I got off the school bus, the house smelled wonderful. Now I'm a homeschooling mom and this recipe is just as convenient for me. My sister says her son and his roommates made this dish while at college too.

1 In a slow cooker, layer potatoes, green beans (draining 2 of the cans) and remaining ingredients.

2 Cover and cook on low setting for 8 hours.

Makes 6 servings

6 potatoes, peeled and cubed

3 14-1/2 oz. cans green beans

1 onion, sliced

1 lb. smoked pork sausage, cut into 2-inch pieces

salt and pepper to taste

ANGEL HAIR BRUNCH FRITTATA

VICKIE
GOOSEBERRY PATCH

Whenever my friends come for brunch, this dish is a must! Very easy to make and you can vary it with veggies and cheeses you have on hand. To double for a potluck, use a 13"x9" baking pan.

8-oz. pkg. angel hair pasta, uncooked

3 eggs, lightly beaten

1/4 c. milk

1/2 c. grated Parmesan cheese

1/2 t. salt

1/8 t. pepper

3/4 c. provolone cheese, shredded

1/2 c. asparagus, chopped

1/2 c. tomato, chopped

1/2 c. sliced black olives, drained

Garnish: tomato and garlic pasta sauce, warmed

1 Cook pasta according to package directions; drain. Meanwhile, in a bowl, whisk together eggs, milk, Parmesan cheese, salt and pepper; mix well. Add cooked pasta to egg mixture; mix gently and spread in a lightly greased 9" pie plate. Top with provolone cheese and vegetables.

2 Cover with aluminum foil. Bake at 350 degrees for 20 minutes. Uncover; bake 15 minutes longer. Cut into wedges and serve warm, topped with pasta sauce.

Makes 6 servings

KITCHEN TIP

Scenic vintage souvenir plates are fun to find at flea markets. They're sure-fire conversation starters at the dinner table too! Look for ones from your home state or from favorite vacation spots.

SLOW-COOKER CHICKEN FAJITAS

KAREN CAMPBELL
CANTON, IL

Serve with a side of black beans & rice and corn chips for a flavorful south-of-the-border feast!

1 Layer half each of peppers, onions, garlic and chicken in a slow cooker; sprinkle with one package taco seasoning and 1/2 teaspoon salt.

2 Repeat layering; drizzle with oil. Cover and cook on low setting for 4 to 6 hours, until chicken is fully cooked and juices run clear. Stir to combine. To serve, spoon chicken mixture onto tortillas, adding desired toppings.

Serves 4 to 6

3 green, yellow or red peppers, sliced

2 onions, sliced

2 T. garlic, finely minced

8 boneless, skinless chicken breasts, cut into thin strips

2 1-1/4 oz. pkgs. taco seasoning mix

1 t. coarse salt, divided

1/2 c. olive oil

8 to 12 flour tortillas

Garnish: salsa, guacamole, sour cream, shredded Colby Jack cheese, chopped black olives, diced tomatoes, shredded lettuce

BRUSCHETTA PIZZA

MADONNA ALEXANDER
CHICAGO, IL

If you can, prepare the bruschetta mix early in the day. The longer the flavor blends, the better it tastes. You'll have some left over but that's okay. I made an omelet with this mix and it was awesome!

10 roma tomatoes, chopped

5 to 6 cloves garlic, minced

2 T. fresh basil, chopped

1/2 red onion, finely chopped

1/4 c. plus 1 T. olive oil, divided

1/2 t. pepper

1/4 t. garlic salt

1/4 c. balsamic vinegar

13.8-oz. tube refrigerated pizza crust dough

1/2 c. pizza sauce

8-oz. pkg. shredded Italian-blend cheese

dried oregano to taste

1 In a large bowl, combine tomatoes, garlic, basil, onion, 1/4 cup oil, pepper, garlic salt and vinegar. Stir to blend; drain. Place pizza crust dough on an ungreased baking sheet.

2 Spread with pizza sauce. Top with 1-1/2 to 2 cups tomato mixture. Sprinkle with cheese and oregano. Drizzle remaining oil over top. Bake according to pizza crust dough package directions.

Serves 6

CITRUS BAKED FISH

DEBRA ARCH
KEWANEE, IL

My kids will eat fish when it's prepared this delicious, easy way.

1 Arrange fresh or thawed fish fillets in a lightly greased 13"x9" baking pan; set aside. In a small skillet, sauté onion and garlic in oil until tender. Stir in parsley, salt and pepper; spoon mixture over fish. Mix orange and lemon juices; drizzle over fish.

2 Cover and bake at 400 degrees for 20 to 25 minutes, until fish flakes easily with a fork. Garnish with paprika and lemon slices.

Serves 4 to 6

6 fillets cod or tilapia, thawed if frozen

1/2 c. onion, finely chopped

2 cloves garlic, minced

2 T. olive oil

2 T. fresh parsley, chopped

1 t. salt

1/8 t. pepper

6-oz. can frozen orange juice concentrate, thawed

1 T. lemon juice

Garnish: paprika, lemon slices

CHAPTER FIVE

NO-FUSS

Snacks & Appetizers

WHETHER YOU ARE HAVING A SPECIAL PARTY OR JUST NEED A SNACK TO TIDE YOU OVER TO THE NEXT MEAL, THESE LITTLE GOODIES ARE SURE TO BECOME FAVORITE GO-TO TREATS.

GOOD MORNING BLUEBERRY SHAKE

JO ANN
GOOSEBERRY PATCH

I enjoy a yummy breakfast shake...this drink blends up fast and is so pretty!

2-1/2 c. blueberries
1-1/4 c. apple juice
1 c. frozen vanilla yogurt
1/4 c. milk
3/4 t. cinnamon
Garnish: additional blueberries

1 Combine all ingredients except garnish in a blender and process until smooth. Garnish with additional blueberries. Serve immediately.

Makes 4 servings

TAM'S TOMATO-BASIL SQUARES

TAMI SEASTROM
BOLINGBROOK, IL

Guests will be wowed by this appetizer pizza!

2 t. all-purpose flour
11-oz. tube refrigerated pizza crust
2 c. shredded mozzarella cheese, divided
1 clove garlic, pressed
2 to 4 plum tomatoes, thinly sliced
1/4 c. shredded Parmesan cheese
2 T. fresh basil, snipped, or 2 t. dried basil
2/3 c. mayonnaise

1 Sprinkle flour on a baking sheet. Spread crust on baking sheet. Sprinkle crust with one cup mozzarella cheese and garlic. Arrange tomato slices in a thin layer over cheese; set aside.

2 In a bowl, combine remaining mozzarella cheese and other ingredients. Mix well; spread evenly over tomatoes. Bake at 375 degrees for 15 to 20 minutes, until bubbly and golden. Cut into squares.

Makes 8 to 12 servings

MEXICAN COFFEE

DELINDA BLAKNEY
BRIDGEVIEW, IL

Stir up this single-serving beverage as dessert after an evening meal...it's sure to satisfy any sweet tooth. The chocolate and hint of cinnamon give the coffee its Mexican origin.

1 Combine first 3 ingredients in a large cup or mug; stir until chocolate melts. Dollop with whipped cream and a cinnamon stick for stirring, if desired.

Makes about 1-1/4 cups

1 c. hot, strong-brewed coffee

1 T. grated semi-sweet chocolate

Optional: 3 T. coffee liqueur

Garnish: whipped cream, cinnamon stick

BONUS IDEA

Serve coffee in mismatched cups and mugs instead of all matched pieces. There will be fun conversation about each interesting cup of coffee.

CHEESY TUNA TRIANGLES

BARB BARGDILL
GOOSEBERRY PATCH

It's the sweet raisin bread and chopped apple that make these little sandwiches stand out from all the rest.

1 T. oil
1 c. apple, cored and chopped
3 T. onion, chopped
7-oz. can tuna, drained
1/4 c. chopped walnuts
1/4 c. mayonnaise
2 t. lemon juice
1/8 t. salt
1/8 t. pepper
4 slices raisin bread, toasted and halved diagonally
4 slices sharp Cheddar cheese, halved diagonally

1 Heat oil in a skillet over medium heat; add apple and onion. Cook, stirring occasionally, about 5 minutes until tender. Remove from heat; transfer to a bowl. Stir in tuna, walnuts, mayonnaise, lemon juice, salt and pepper. Place toast slices on an ungreased baking sheet. Top with tuna mixture and a slice of cheese.

2 Broil 4 to 5 inches from heat for 3 to 4 minutes, or until cheese begins to melt. Cut into triangles.

Makes 16

SYCAMORE FARM CHRISTMAS DRINK

PENNY ARNOLD
LOUISVILLE, IL

The holidays are near when I begin making this drink at our family home in the country, appropriately named Sycamore Farm.

1 Combine all ingredients except garnish in a large stockpot over medium heat. Stir often until heated through. Remove cloves.

2 Garnish with orange slices and cinnamon sticks.

Makes 16 cups

64-oz. bottle cranberry juice

64-oz. bottle apple juice

1/2 c. orange juice

1 T. cinnamon

1 T. whole cloves

2/3 c. sugar

Garnish: orange slices and cinnamon sticks

ILLINOIS FUN FACT

Talk about fusion cooking. In reality, Pizza Puffs are small folded versions of pizza flavors wrapped in a tortilla and deep fried. They are popular at fast-food spots and come in various flavors, plus a breakfast version.

ENCHILADA DIPPIN' RICE

MADONNA ALEXANDER
CHICAGO, IL

A quick and fun Mexican meal! We love watching football games on television. On game nights I try to make something fun to eat. This dish can be made ahead and just heated up later.

1-1/2 to 2 lbs. ground beef or turkey

10-oz. can mild red enchilada sauce

10-3/4 oz. can Cheddar cheese soup

2 c. cooked brown or white rice

16-oz. can refried beans, warmed

16-oz. pkg. shredded Mexican-blend cheese

Garnish: salsa, sour cream, guacamole

Optional: canned sweet corn & diced peppers, chopped black olives and jalapeño peppers

scoop-type tortilla or corn chips

1 In a large skillet over medium heat, cook beef or turkey until no longer pink; drain. Add sauce and soup; heat through. Add cooked rice; mix well and remove from heat.

2 Spread beans to cover the bottom of a lightly greased 13"x9" baking pan. Spread meat mixture on top; cover with cheese. Let stand for several minutes, until cheese melts. Garnish as desired; serve with chips for dipping. May also be served as a casserole, with chips crushed and spread on top.

Serves 6 to 8

JUST PEACHY FREEZER JAM

SHERRY GORDON
ARLINGTON HEIGHTS, IL

For a yummy appetizer, spread crackers with cream cheese and dollop with jam.

1 Combine peaches, sugar and lemon juice in a large bowl; set aside 10 minutes, stirring occasionally. Mix water and pectin in a saucepan. Bring to a boil over high heat, stirring constantly. Continue boiling and stirring one minute; add to peach mixture, stirring until sugar is dissolved.

2 Spoon into sterilized containers, leaving 1/2-inch headspace; secure lids. Let stand at room temperature 24 hours. Jam is now ready to freeze. Thaw in refrigerator before using.

Makes 6 containers

3 c. peaches, pitted, peeled and finely chopped

4-1/2 c. sugar

2 T. lemon juice

3/4 c. water

1-3/4 oz. pkg. powdered pectin

6 1/2-pint freezer-safe plastic containers and lids, sterilized

MINI TURKEY-BERRY BITES

JACKIE SMULSKI
LYONS, IL

Everybody will gobble these hearty "sandwiches" right up!

2 c. biscuit baking mix
1/2 c. sweetened dried cranberries
1 c. milk
2 T. Dijon mustard
1 egg, beaten
6-oz. pkg. thinly sliced smoked turkey, chopped and divided
3/4 c. shredded Swiss cheese, divided

1 Stir together baking mix, cranberries, milk, mustard and egg until blended. Pour half the batter into a lightly greased 8"x8" baking pan.

2 Arrange half the turkey over batter; sprinkle half the cheese nearly to edges of pan. Top with remaining turkey, followed by remaining batter.

3 Bake, uncovered, at 350 degrees for 45 to 50 minutes, until golden and set. Sprinkle with remaining cheese; let stand 5 minutes. To serve, cut into 9 squares; slice each square diagonally.

Makes 1-1/2 dozen

BONUS IDEA

Choosing the perfect avocado can be daunting. The avocado should be firm but yield to gentle pressure and it should have a slightly bumpy texture. Color can vary, but usually the darker ones are riper.

PEANUT BUTTER-HONEY SPREAD

MARY SCHROCK
SEATON, IL

This tastes absolutely great on toast!

1 Beat all ingredients together until fluffy. Spoon into an airtight container; cover and keep refrigerated.

Makes 1-1/2 cups

1/4 c. creamy peanut butter
2 T. butter, softened
1/2 c. powdered sugar
1/3 c. honey
1/4 t. cinnamon

VICKIE'S FAVORITE GUACAMOLE

VICKIE
GOOSEBERRY PATCH

Whenever we have a Mexican-themed potluck, I'm requested to bring my homemade guacamole. It's almost foolproof and oh-so-good!

1 Scoop pulp out of avocados into a bowl. Mash to desired consistency with a potato masher. Add remaining ingredients; mix well. Serve with your favorite tortilla chips.

Makes 2 cups

4 avocados, halved and pitted
1 onion, chopped
2 cloves garlic, minced
2 T. lime juice
1/8 t. kosher salt
tortilla chips

CARAMEL CEREAL MIX TREAT

JENNIFER SEALS
QUINCY, IL

Once you start snacking on this, you can't stop! So quick & easy to make. Perfect for fall treat bags or tucking into lunchboxes.

12-oz. pkg. corn & rice cereal
16-oz. jar dry-roasted peanuts
3/4 c. butter
1-1/2 c. brown sugar, packed
1/2 c. corn syrup
1 t. baking soda

1 Combine cereal and peanuts in a large microwave-safe bowl; set aside.

2 In a heavy saucepan over medium heat, combine butter, brown sugar and corn syrup. Cook until butter melts; bring to a gentle boil, stirring frequently. Boil for 2 minutes. Remove saucepan from heat and stir in baking soda.

3 Pour butter mixture over cereal mixture; stir to coat. Microwave on high for 6 minutes, stirring every 2 minutes until cereal is well coated. Pour onto lightly greased baking sheets. Cool; break apart and store in an airtight container.

Makes about 17 cups

GREAT-AUNT LAURA'S CHEESE

KATE KELLY GALLEGOS
AURORA, IL

In our family, this recipe is legendary! We love it so much, we eat it out of the bowl with a spoon, but it's delicious as a dip with any kind of chips. We always double it because everyone wants a huge bowl for themselves...it's really that good!

1 Combine all ingredients together in a large bowl. Beat with an electric mixer on low speed until smooth. Cover and keep refrigerated.

Serves 4 to 8

16-oz. container cottage cheese
8-oz. container sour cream
3-oz. pkg. cream cheese, softened
2 T. milk
1 clove garlic, pressed
salt to taste

CHICKEN-SALSA DIP

MARGARET COLLINS
CLARENDON HILLS, IL

Scoop it out with tortilla chips or corn chips...a perfect appetizer for a small gathering!

1 Blend cream cheese with half of the salsa; spread in the bottom of an ungreased 9" pie plate. Top with remaining salsa; sprinkle with cheese and chicken.

2 Bake, uncovered, at 350 degrees for 25 minutes, until hot and cheese is melted. Serve warm with tortilla chips.

Serves 8

8-oz. pkg. cream cheese, softened
8-oz. jar salsa, divided
8-oz. pkg. shredded Mexican-blend cheese
2 to 3 boneless, skinless chicken breasts, cooked and diced
tortilla chips

PINK LASSIES

SUSAN MAURER
DAHLGREN, IL

When I was growing up, I used to request this fruity beverage often. It's still delightful and makes a refreshing summertime treat.

1 c. cranberry juice cocktail
1/4 c. orange juice
1 c. vanilla ice cream

1 Combine all ingredients in a blender. Cover and blend until smooth. Serve in tall glasses with straws.

Makes 2 servings

PLEASING PIZZA DIP

JENNIFER CRISP
ABINGDON, IL

This recipe goes so fast that I have to put out two slow cookers for our family gatherings! You can toss in any of your favorite pizza toppings, and it will be delicious.

1 c. ground Italian pork sausage, browned and drained
1 c. pepperoni, diced
2 8-oz. pkgs. cream cheese, cubed
2 c. shredded Cheddar cheese
1-1/2 c. sour cream
2-1/2 c. pizza sauce
2 to 3 T. dried oregano
2 t. garlic powder
tortilla chips

1 Combine all ingredients except tortilla chips in a slow cooker. Cover and cook on low setting for 2 hours, stirring occasionally, until dip is smooth and warmed through. Serve warm with tortilla chips.

Serves 10 to 12

WORLD'S BEST COCKTAIL MEATBALLS

GINA LIVOLSI NORTON
WONDER LAKE, IL

This recipe has been in our family for over 50 years. They are the best cocktail meatballs anyone has ever tasted. Just set out a crock of these and watch them disappear...enjoy!

1 In a bowl, combine beef, cereal, milk, 1/4 cup chili sauce, Worcestershire sauce, onion and salt; mix well. Cover and refrigerate for 30 minutes. Form beef mixture into walnut-size balls. Place meatballs on a baking sheet; bake at 375 degrees for 20 minutes, or until browned.

2 Transfer meatballs to a slow cooker; set aside. In a saucepan over medium heat, combine remaining chili sauce and grape jelly. Cook and stir until jelly is melted; spoon over meatballs and stir gently. Set slow cooker to low setting for serving; heat through.

Serves 10

1 lb. ground beef chuck
1/2 c. corn flake cereal, crushed
1/2 c. evaporated milk
12-oz. bottle chili sauce, divided
1 T. Worcestershire sauce
1/4 c. onion, finely chopped
1 t. salt
10-oz. jar grape jelly

CHAPTER SIX

TIME-FOR-A-TREAT
Desserts

YOU WOULDN'T DREAM OF ENDING

A MEAL WITHOUT JUST A TASTE

OF SOMETHING SWEET, AND THESE

DELICIOUS DISHES ARE SURE TO

PUT THE ICING ON THE CAKE.

GRANDMA'S KOLACHY COOKIES

JENNIFER SAVINO
JOLLIET, IL

My grandma would bake trays of cookies every Christmas to give to each family. She used an array of jams she preserved from her garden as the Kolachy filling. My favorite was her raspberry jam. These cookies take a bit more effort than other cookies, but the end result is worth it. I hope you enjoy these as much as I do!

1 t. active dry yeast
2 T. warm water
2-1/2 c. all-purpose flour
1 T. sugar
1/2 t. salt
1 c. butter, softened
2 T. whipping cream, scalded and cooled
4 egg yolks, beaten
18-oz. jar raspberry jam

1 Dissolve yeast in warm water, about 110 to 115 degrees. In a separate bowl, sift together flour, sugar and salt. Cut in butter until coarse crumbs form. Mix in yeast mixture, cream and egg yolks. Cover and chill for several hours.

2 On a lightly floured surface, roll dough to about 1/2-inch thick. Cut with a 2-inch round cookie cutter. Cover and let rise until double in size. Place on lightly greased baking sheets. Make a depression in center of each cookie and fill with jam. Bake at 350 degrees for 15 minutes.

Makes about 3 dozen

BROWN SUGAR PINEAPPLE CRISP

ARLENE SMULSKI
LYONS, IL

Fresh pineapple is my very favorite fruit! This baked crisp combines a tantalizing taste of paradise, while fresh ginger balances out the sweetness. Top with whipped cream or pineapple sorbet...yum!

1 Place pineapple in a bowl; set aside. In a separate bowl, combine brown sugar, flour, oats, nutmeg and salt. With your fingers, rub in butter until coarse crumbs form and mixture holds together when squeezed. Cover and chill while making filling.

2 In a small bowl, whisk together lime juice and ginger; stir into pineapple. Sprinkle cornstarch over pineapple; stir again. Transfer pineapple mixture to a lightly greased 9"x9" glass baking pan. Sprinkle crumb mixture and coconut evenly over top. Cover with aluminum foil.

3 Bake at 375 degrees for 20 minutes. Uncover; bake about 10 minutes more, until bubbly around the edges and top is crisp and golden. Cool 10 to 15 minutes before serving.

Makes 8 servings

1 pineapple, peeled, cored and cubed
1/2 c. brown sugar, packed
1/2 c. all-purpose flour
1/4 c. long-cooking oats, uncooked
1/8 t. nutmeg
1/2 t. salt
1/4 c. butter, diced
1 T. lime juice
1 T. fresh ginger, peeled and grated
1 T. cornstarch
1/3 c. sweetened flaked coconut

BUTTERSCOTCH FONDUE

**SHERRY GORDON
ARLINGTON HEIGHTS, IL**

*In a word, irresistible! This smooth, warm butterscotch
makes a wonderful topping for ice cream or cake too.*

2 14-oz. cans sweetened
   condensed milk

2 c. brown sugar, packed

1 c. butter, melted

2/3 c. light corn syrup

1 t. vanilla extract

1/4 c. rum or milk

sponge cake or brownie
   cubes, sliced apples,
   whole strawberries,
   small cookies

1 In a 4-quart slow cooker, combine condensed
milk, brown sugar, butter, corn syrup and vanilla.

2 Cover and cook on low setting for 3 hours.
Whisk in rum or milk until smooth. Keep warm
on low setting for serving up to 2 hours, stirring
occasionally. Serve with desired dippers.

Makes about 5 cups

JOYCE'S CHOCOLATE CHIP PIE

JOYCE TIMKO
GRANITE CITY, IL

Chocolate, butter and whipped cream...oh, my!

1 In a bowl, mix eggs, flour, sugars, pecans and melted butter until well blended. Sprinkle chocolate chips in unbaked pie crust. Pour egg mixture over top.

2 Bake at 350 degrees for 45 to 50 minutes, until golden. Pie will become firm as it cools. Garnish as desired.

Serves 8

2 eggs, beaten
1/4 c. all-purpose flour
1/3 c. sugar
1-1/2 c. brown sugar, packed
1 c. chopped pecans
1/2 c. butter, melted and cooled slightly
3/4 c. mini semi-sweet chocolate chips
9-inch pie crust
Optional: whipped cream, additional mini chocolate chips

ILLINOIS FUN FACT

Twinkies. Who knew they were developed in Chicago about 1930? The spongy yellow snack cake was first stuffed with banana filling, but later the vanilla filling stuck. How many of those did you carry in your school lunch back in the day? A number of state fairs now offer deep-fried Twinkies.

HOMEMADE CARAMEL SAUCE

GRETCHEN HICKMAN
GALVA, IL

This sauce is delicious! My great-aunt owned an apple orchard for many years, so she really knew her apple desserts. Serve this sauce for dipping apples or drizzle it over sliced apples and apple desserts.

14-oz. can sweetened
condensed milk
1/2 c. butter, sliced
2 c. brown sugar, packed
3/4 c. light corn syrup
1/8 t. salt

1 Combine all ingredients in a heavy saucepan over medium heat. Bring to a boil, stirring constantly.

2 Cover and cook for about 5 minutes, until mixture reaches the soft-ball stage, or 234 to 243 degrees on a candy thermometer. Transfer into a mini slow cooker on low setting for serving. Cover and refrigerate any leftovers.

Makes about 2 cups

SOFT PEANUT BUTTER COOKIES

BRENDA TRANKA
AMBOY, IL

If you're a peanut butter fan, these cookies won't last long. You'll enjoy every last crumb! Don't forget to serve them with a tall, cold glass of milk.

1 c. sugar
1 c. creamy peanut
butter
1 egg, slightly beaten
1 t. vanilla extract

1 Combine all ingredients; mix well. Roll dough into one-inch balls and place on an ungreased baking sheet. Use a fork to press a crisscross pattern into the top of each cookie.

2 Bake at 325 degrees for 10 minutes or until golden. Let cool before removing from sheet.

Makes 2 dozen

PINEAPPLE-NUT COOKIES

**NORMA LONGNECKER
LAWRENCEVILLE, IL**

I've enjoyed these cookies for years. I began making them when my children were small, and now I make them for my grandkids.

1 Beat butter and brown sugar until light and fluffy; blend in egg. Combine flour and baking soda. Add to butter mixture; blend well. Stir in pecans, pineapple and vanilla; drop by teaspoonfuls onto ungreased baking sheets.

2 Bake at 375 degrees for 10 to 12 minutes. Cool on wire racks. Drizzle with thin frosting if desired.

Makes about 3-1/2 dozen, serves 42

1/2 c. butter, softened

1/3 c. brown sugar, packed

1 egg

2-1/2 c. all-purpose flour

1 t. baking soda

1/2 c. pecans, chopped

8-oz. can crushed pineapple in own juice, drained

1/2 t. vanilla extract

Optional: thin frosting

BONUS IDEA

Instead of serving cookies on small plates, make the cookies a bit smaller and serve the sweet gems in paper cups.

NO-BAKE GRANOLA BARS

PATRICE LINDSEY
LOCKPORT, IL

Try other dried fruit like blueberries or raisins too!

1/4 c. coconut oil, divided
1 c. creamy peanut butter
1/2 c. honey
2 c. long-cooking oats, uncooked
2 c. crispy rice cereal
1 c. sweetened flaked coconut
1/2 c. dried cranberries, chopped
1/2 c. mini semi-sweet chocolate chips

1 Lightly grease a 13"x9" baking pan with a small amount of coconut oil; set aside. In a large saucepan, combine remaining coconut oil, peanut butter and honey.

2 Cook and stir over low heat just until blended and smooth. Remove from heat; add oats, cereal, coconut and cranberries. Stir just until evenly coated and well combined. Let cool about 10 minutes; stir in chocolate chips.

3 Quickly transfer mixture to baking pan; spread evenly with a spatula. Cover with plastic wrap or wax paper; press mixture down evenly and firmly. Refrigerate for one hour before cutting into bars. May be kept tightly covered and refrigerated for up to 10 days.

Makes 16 bars

OATMEAL-CARROT COOKIES

DIANA CARLILE
CHATHAM, IL

These chewy cookies are my family's favorites!

1 Beat margarine until soft. Add sugars and 1/2 cup flour; mix well. Add remaining ingredients except oats, carrots and raisins. Beat well.

2 Add remaining flour; mix well. Stir in oats, carrots and raisins, if using. Drop by rounded teaspoonfuls onto ungreased baking sheets. Bake at 375 degrees for 10 minutes.

Makes 3 dozen

3/4 c. margarine
3/4 c. brown sugar, packed
1/2 c. sugar
13/4 c. all-purpose flour, divided
1 egg, beaten
1 t. baking powder
1/4 t. baking soda
1/2 t. cinnamon
1 t. vanilla extract
2 c. quick-cooking oats, uncooked
1 c. carrots, peeled and shredded
Optional: 1/2 c. raisins

BONUS IDEA

Old road maps make fun placemats. Family members can share memories of trips they've taken or daydream about places they'd like to go. Simply cut maps to placemat size, then top with postcards, ticket stubs or clippings and seal in self-adhesive clear plastic.

PEANUT BUTTER SURPRISE COOKIES

SHERRY GORDON
ARLINGTON HEIGHTS, IL

Yum, yum, yum! I like to divvy up the dough between baking sheets and chill the second batch while the first is baking.

16-1/2 oz. tube refrigerated peanut butter cookie dough
12 mini peanut butter cups
1/3 c. semi-sweet chocolate chips
1 t. shortening

1 Divide cookie dough into 12 pieces. With floured fingers, wrap one piece of dough around each peanut butter cup. Place on ungreased baking sheets.

2 Bake at 350 degrees for 10 to 15 minutes, until golden. Cool on baking sheets one minute; remove to wire rack to cool completely. In a saucepan, melt chocolate chips and shortening over low heat, stirring constantly. Drizzle melted chocolate over cookies. Let stand until set.

Makes one dozen

PEPPERMINT ICE CREAM

TORI WILLIS
CHAMPAIGN, IL

Christmas to me: sitting in front of the Christmas tree after decorating it, my mum sitting in my dad's lap, Christmas carols on the radio, us kids lined up on the couch each with a bowl of peppermint ice cream, no one saying a word, just admiring the glow of the pretty lights and the twinkle of tinsel...magical!

1 Whisk together milk and sugar until sugar is completely dissolved. Add cream and extracts. Pour into an ice cream maker.

2 Churn about 20 to 25 minutes according to manufacturer's instructions, until thick and creamy. Add candy canes; churn an additional 5 minutes.

Makes 1-1/2 quarts

1 c. milk
2/3 c. sugar
2 c. whipping cream
1/2 t. vanilla extract
1/2 t. peppermint extract
2/3 c. candy canes, crushed

BONUS IDEA

Take it easy and have a leftovers night once a week. Set out yummy leftovers so everyone can choose their favorite. End with cookies and ice cream for dessert. What could be simpler?

CANDY APPLE CHEESECAKE

SHERRY GORDON
ARLINGTON HEIGHTS, IL

My family loves to have a big slice of this after a hearty fall meal, but it's delicious any time of year.

21-oz. can apple pie filling, divided
9-inch graham cracker crust
2 8-oz. pkgs. cream cheese, softened
1/2 c. sugar
1/2 t. vanilla extract
2 eggs, beaten
1/2 c. caramel ice cream topping
12 pecan halves
2 T. chopped pecans

1 Reserve 1/2 cup apple pie filling; spoon remaining filling into crust. In a bowl, beat together cream cheese, sugar and vanilla until smooth. Add eggs and beat well; pour over filling.

2 Bake at 350 degrees for 35 minutes, or until center is set; cool. Combine caramel topping and reserved apple pie filling in a small saucepan; cook and stir over medium heat for about one minute.

3 Spoon caramel mixture evenly over cheesecake. Arrange pecan halves around edge; sprinkle with chopped pecans. Keep chilled until serving.

Serves 8 to 12

COFFEE CREAM BROWNIES

JENNIFER CRISP
ABINGDON, IL

Go ahead and serve with a scoop of ice cream...so good!

1 In a saucepan over low heat, melt baking chocolate and 1/2 cup butter; let cool. In a bowl, beat eggs, sugar and vanilla. Stir in chocolate mixture.

2 Combine flour and baking soda and add to the chocolate mixture. Spread in a greased 8"x8" baking pan.

3 Bake at 350 degrees for 25 to 30 minutes. Let cool. In a bowl, stir coffee granules into one tablespoon cream until dissolved. Beat in remaining butter and powdered sugar until creamy; spread over brownies.

4 In a saucepan over low heat, stir and melt chocolate chips and remaining cream until thickened. Spread over cream layer. Let set and cut into squares.

Makes one dozen

3 1-oz. sqs. unsweetened baking chocolate, chopped

1/2 c. plus 2 T. butter, softened and divided

2 eggs, beaten

1 c. sugar

1 t. vanilla extract

2/3 c. all-purpose flour

1/4 t. baking soda

1 t. instant coffee granules

1/3 c. plus 1 T. whipping cream, divided

1 c. powdered sugar

1 c. semi-sweet chocolate chips

CRUNCHY OAT & FRUIT CRISP

SANDI FIGURA
DECATUR, IL

A crunchy, fruit-filled crisp that's tasty warm or cold.

1 c. quick-cooking oats, uncooked

3/4 c. brown sugar, packed and divided

5 T. all-purpose flour, divided

1/3 c. margarine, melted

1 c. blueberries

1 c. cherries, pitted

4 apples, peeled, cored and thickly sliced

1/4 c. frozen orange juice concentrate, thawed

1 T. cinnamon

1 In a bowl, combine oats, 1/2 cup brown sugar, 2 tablespoons flour and margarine; set aside.

2 In a separate bowl, combine fruit, 1/4 cup remaining brown sugar and other ingredients. Stir until fruit is evenly coated.

3 Spoon fruit mixture into an ungreased 8"x8" baking pan. Sprinkle oat mixture over top.

4 Bake at 350 degrees for 30 to 35 minutes, until apples are tender and topping is golden.

Serves 4 to 6

FROSTED CHERRY DROPS

CHARLENE SIDWELL
ALTAMONT, IL

These have always been a favorite of our family. They're perfect for a colorful plate of cookies, either for home or as a gift.

1 In a bowl, combine dry cake mix, sour cream, cherry juice, almond extract and egg. Fold in chopped cherries.

2 Drop by teaspoonfuls, 2 inches apart, onto ungreased baking sheets. Bake at 350 degrees for 8 to 12 minutes, until edges are lightly golden. Cool one minute on baking sheets; remove to a wire rack to cool completely. Frost with Cherry Frosting; top with cherry quarters.

Makes 2-1/2 to 3 dozen

18-1/2 oz. pkg. white cake mix

1/2 c. sour cream

3 T. maraschino cherry juice

1/4 t. almond extract

1 egg, beaten

1/2 c. maraschino cherries, finely chopped

Garnish: maraschino cherries, quartered

1 In a small bowl, combine all ingredients, adding enough milk for desired spreading consistency.

CHERRY FROSTING

2-1/2 c. powdered sugar

1/4 c. butter, softened

1 T. maraschino cherry juice

2 to 3 T. milk

RED VELVET CAKE BALLS

TORI WILLIS
CHAMPAIGN, IL

These are so fun and easy to make. Let the kids help make 'em!

18-1/2 oz. pkg. red velvet cake mix

16-oz. container cream cheese frosting

16-oz. pkg. regular or white melting chocolate

1 Prepare and bake cake mix following package directions for a 13"x9" cake; let cool. Crumble cooled cake into a large bowl. Stir in cream cheese frosting. Roll mixture into balls the size of quarters. Place on baking sheets and chill for several hours or overnight. Melt chocolate in a double boiler. Dip cake balls into chocolate and place on wax paper. Let sit until firm.

Makes about 4 dozen

SPICED CRANBERRY-APPLE CRISP

ARLENE SMULSKI
LYONS, IL

I have made this fall dessert many times and it never fails. No matter what kind of apples you use, it will come out perfectly!

4 Golden Delicious apples, peeled, cored and sliced

1 c. fresh cranberries

3/4 c. light brown sugar, packed

1/2 c. all-purpose flour

1/2 c. rolled oats, uncooked

3/4 t. cinnamon

3/4 t. nutmeg

1/3 c. butter, softened

Garnish: ice cream or whipped cream

1 Combine apples and cranberries in a buttered 8"x8" baking pan; set aside. In a bowl, combine remaining ingredients except garnish. Mix well and sprinkle over fruit.

2 Bake at 375 degrees for 30 minutes, or until top is golden. Serve warm; garnish with ice cream or whipped cream.

Makes 6 servings

SALTED NUT ROLL BARS

SANDY GROEZINGER
STOCKTON, IL

Salty, sweet, crunchy and gooey...every bite satisfies!

1 Combine dry cake mix, egg and melted butter; press into a greased 13"x9" baking pan.

2 Bake at 350 degrees for 10 to 12 minutes. Sprinkle marshmallows over baked crust; return to oven and bake for 3 additional minutes, or until marshmallows are melted.

3 In a saucepan over medium heat, melt peanut butter chips, corn syrup, butter and vanilla. Stir in nuts and cereal. Spread mixture over marshmallow layer. Chill briefly until firm; cut into squares.

Makes 2-1/2 dozen

18-1/2 oz. pkg. yellow
 cake mix
1 egg, beaten
1/4 c. butter, melted and
 slightly cooled
3 c. mini marshmallows
10-oz. pkg. peanut butter
 chips
1/2 c. light corn syrup
1/2 c. butter, softened
1 t. vanilla extract
2 c. salted peanuts
2 c. crispy rice cereal

AUTUMN APPLE MILKSHAKE

**VICKIE
GOOSEBERRY PATCH**

This cool treat really hits the spot after a long session of raking leaves!

14-oz. can sweetened
condensed milk
1 c. applesauce
1/2 c. apple cider
1/2 t. apple pie spice
3 c. crushed ice
Garnish: cinnamon

1 In a blender, combine all ingredients except ice and cinnamon. Gradually add ice, blending until smooth. Garnish with cinnamon.

Serves 4 to 6

PUMPKIN PIE PUDDING

**LANA RULEVISH
ASHLEY, IL**

I received this recipe from a friend I met online. It is very good!

15-oz. can pumpkin
12-oz. can evaporated
milk
3/4 c. sugar
1/2 c. biscuit baking mix
2 eggs, beaten
2 T. butter, melted
2-1/2 t. pumpkin pie
spice
2 t. vanilla extract
Garnish: whipped cream

1 In a bowl, mix together all ingredients except topping. Transfer to a slow cooker that has been sprayed with non-stick vegetable spray.

2 Cover and cook on low setting for 3-1/2 to 4 hours. Pudding will start to pull away from sides of slow cooker; test for doneness with a toothpick inserted in center. Serve warm, topped with dollops of whipped cream.

Makes 4 to 6 servings

CHOCOLATE-MINT DESSERT

CARLA TERPSTRA
ROCKPORT, IL

This is beautiful garnished with mint leaves and crushed peppermint sticks.

1 Combine flour, butter and pecans; press into a greased 13"x9" pan. Bake at 350 degrees for 30 minutes.

2 Beat cream cheese, powdered sugar, peppermint flavoring, food coloring and about 2/3 of the whipped topping together. Spread over cooled crust. Combine pudding with milk. Pour over cream cheese layer.

3 Spread remaining whipped topping over all. Refrigerate before serving.

Makes 12 servings

1-1/2 c. all-purpose flour
3/4 c. butter
2/3 c. chopped pecans
8-oz. pkg. cream cheese, softened
1 c. powdered sugar
1 t. peppermint flavoring
green food coloring as desired
12-oz. container frozen whipped topping, thawed and divided
2 3-1/2 oz. pkg's. instant chocolate pudding mix
3 c. milk

CINNAMON BREAD PUDDING

**JUSTINE DILLON
CHARLESTON, IL**

This is an absolutely fabulous dessert!

12 c. cinnamon bread, torn
1 c. raisins
1 t. cinnamon-sugar
6 eggs, beaten
6 c. milk
1 c. sugar
1 c. water
4 T. butter, melted
2 t. vanilla extract
1 c. sugar
2 T. cornstarch

1 Place bread into a greased 13"x9" baking pan; scatter raisins over bread and sprinkle cinnamon-sugar over all. In a separate bowl, combine eggs, milk and sugar; blend well. Pour over bread. Press bread down with a fork until bread is soaked.

2 Bake at 350 degrees for one hour or until set. In a saucepan over medium heat, bring water to a boil; add butter and vanilla. Mix sugar and cornstarch together and add to mixture in saucepan. Cook over low heat until semi-thick, stirring frequently. Pour sauce over bread pudding and serve warm.

Makes 10 to 12 servings

CREAM PUFFS

JANE GRANGER
MANTENO, IL

When I make this dessert, I have to make two because my daughter wants to take one home!

1 In a saucepan, bring water and butter to a boil; remove from heat. Add flour and beat with a fork until it forms a ball. Transfer to a bowl; add eggs, one at a time, beating well after each. Pour and spread into a 15"x11" jelly-roll pan.

2 Bake at 400 degrees for 25 to 30 minutes; cool. Poke holes with a toothpick in pastry while baking to let the air out. In another bowl, beat cream cheese with an electric mixer at medium speed until smooth. Add dry pudding mix and milk; beat until blended.

3 Spread mixture evenly over pastry. When ready to serve, spread whipped topping over pudding layer and drizzle with chocolate syrup.

Makes 10 to 12 servings

1 c. water
1/2 c. butter
1 c. all-purpose flour
4 eggs
8-oz. pkg. cream cheese, softened
2 3-1/2 oz. pkgs. instant vanilla pudding mix
4 c. milk
8-oz. container frozen whipped topping, thawed
chocolate syrup to taste

NELLIE'S PERSIMMON COOKIES

**DOROTHY AMES
LERNA, IL**

*A ripe persimmon should be soft to the touch and yield between
1/2 to 3/4 cup of pulp.*

1 persimmon
1 c. butter, softened
1 c. brown sugar, packed
1 c. sugar
2 eggs, beaten
2-1/2 c. all-purpose flour
1/2 t. baking soda
1 c. chopped pecans

1 Rinse persimmon under cold water; pat dry. Using a small sharp knife, make an X-shaped cut in the pointed end. Pull back sections of peel from cut end; discard seeds, peel and stem end. Process pulp in food processor or blender until smooth. Reserve 1/2 cup persimmon pulp purée; save any remaining pulp purée for another use.

2 Beat butter and sugars in a large bowl with an electric mixer at medium speed until light and fluffy. Beat in eggs and persimmon pulp. Combine flour and baking soda in a separate bowl, stirring to mix; gradually add flour mixture to butter mixture, beating until blended. Fold in pecans; cover and chill one hour.

3 Drop by teaspoonfuls onto ungreased baking sheets. Press each cookie with a fork dipped in warm water. Bake at 350 degrees for 10 minutes, or until golden. Remove to wire racks to cool. Store in an airtight container.

Makes 6 dozen

PEPPERMINT BARK BROWNIES

ANGIE BIGGIN
LYONS, IL

Using a brownie mix makes these so easy to make and so yummy!

1 Prepare and bake brownie mix in a lightly greased 13"x9" baking pan according to package directions. Cool completely in pan on a wire rack.

2 Combine chocolate chips and butter in a saucepan; heat over low heat until melted, stirring constantly with a rubber spatula. Spread chocolate mixture over brownies; sprinkle with crushed candy. Let stand 30 minutes, or until frosting hardens. Cut into squares; store in an airtight container.

Makes 2 dozen

20-oz. pkg. fudge
  brownie mix
12-oz. pkg. white
  chocolate chips
2 t. butter
1-1/2 c. candy canes,
  crushed

ILLINOIS FUN FACT

Cracker Jack, candied popcorn mixed with peanuts, was introduced at the 1893 World's Fair and soon became a ballpark staple. In 1908, the treat took hold when it became a part of the song "Take Me Out to the Ballgame." Its future was sealed. Little prizes were added in 1912 and remain today. Flavors other than the original now are options.

INDEX

INDEX continued

U.S. to METRIC RECIPE EQUIVALENTS

Volume Measurements

¼ teaspoon . . . . 1 mL
½ teaspoon . . . . 2 mL
1 teaspoon . . . . 5 mL
1 tablespoon = 3 teaspoons . . . . . . 15 mL
2 tablespoons = 1 fluid ounce . . . . 30 mL
¼ cup . . . . 60 mL
⅓ cup . . . . 75 mL
½ cup = 4 fluid ounces . . . . 125 mL
1 cup = 8 fluid ounces . . . . 250 mL
2 cups = 1 pint = 16 fluid ounces 500 mL
4 cups = 1 quart . . . . 1 L

Weights

1 ounce . . . . 30 g
4 ounces . . . . 120 g
8 ounces . . . . 225 g
16 ounces = 1 pound . . . . 450 g

Baking Pan Sizes

Square
8x8x2 inches . . . . 2 L = 20x20x5 cm
9x9x2 inches . . . . . . 2.5 L = 23x23x5 cm

Rectangular
13x9x2 inches . . . . . 3.5 L = 33x23x5 cm

Loaf
9x5x3 inches . . . . 2 L = 23x13x7 cm

Round
8x1½ inches . . . . 1.2 L = 20x4 cm
9x1½ inches . . . . 1.5 L = 23x4 cm

Recipe Abbreviations

t. = teaspoon . . . . ltr. = liter
T. = tablespoon . . . . oz. = ounce
c. = cup . . . . lb. = pound
pt. = pint . . . . doz. = dozen
qt. = quart . . . . .pkg. = package
gal. = gallon . . . . env. = envelope

Oven Temperatures

300° F . . . . .150° C
325° F . . . . .160° C
350° F . . . . .180° C
375° F . . . . .190° C
400° F . . . . .200° C
450° F . . . . .230° C

Kitchen Measurements

A pinch = ⅛ tablespoon
1 fluid ounce = 2 tablespoons
3 teaspoons = 1 tablespoon
4 fluid ounces = ½ cup
2 tablespoons = ⅛ cup
8 fluid ounces = 1 cup
4 tablespoons = ¼ cup
16 fluid ounces = 1 pint
8 tablespoons = ½ cup
32 fluid ounces = 1 quart
16 tablespoons = 1 cup
16 ounces net weight = 1 pound
2 cups = 1 pint
4 cups = 1 quart
4 quarts = 1 gallon

Send us your favorite recipe

and the memory that makes it special for you!*

If we select your recipe for a brand-new **Gooseberry Patch** cookbook, your name will appear right along with it...and you'll receive a FREE copy of the book!

Submit your recipe on our website at

www.gooseberrypatch.com/sharearecipe

*Please include the number of servings and all other necessary information.

Have a taste for more?

Visit www.gooseberrypatch.com to join our Circle of Friends!

• Free recipes, tips and ideas plus a complete cookbook index
• Get mouthwatering recipes and special email offers delivered to your inbox.

You'll also love these cookbooks from **Gooseberry Patch**!

5-Ingredient Family Favorite Recipes
America's Comfort Foods
Best Church Suppers
Best-Ever Cookie, Brownie & Bar Recipes
Best-Ever Sheet Pan & Skillet Recipes
Cozy Christmas Comforts
Delicious Recipes for Diabetics
Harvest Homestyle Meals
Healthy, Happy, Homemade Meals
Meals in Minutes: 15, 20, 30

www.gooseberrypatch.com